WHAT OTHERS ARE SAYING

"I should have read this book two husbands ago!"

—*Wanda Graham, Homemaker*

"This read is a dose of good common sense sprinkled with humor and a pinch of reality."

—*Vetta Holman, Counseling & Wellness,*
UNC–Chapel Hill

"At the end of the day, this stuff will save your relationship."

—*Debby James, Attorney*

"Mr. or Ms. JUST Right is a mirror for me to view myself as I am and to accept others as they present themselves to me."

—*Utibe Edoh, Student of Psychology*

"Finally! Someone who tells us the truths about making relationships work!"

—*Lia Sheplin, Writer*

"ART (Acceptance, Respect, and Trust) is the best! It has brought balance in my relationships with family, friends and my church congregation."

—*Jen Lawrence, Pastor*

"If everyone listened to Oprah, half the Divorce lawyers in this country would be out of business."

—*J. T. Krutz, Divorce Attorney*

"When my fifteen-year-old son was being pressured by his girlfriend to lose his virginity, I pulled him aside and told him about Acceptance, Respect, and Trust (ART). Our conversation brought us closer together and kept him from making a huge mistake."

—*Sandra Janson, Teacher*

MR. OR MS. JUST RIGHT

MR. OR MS. JUST RIGHT

• SECOND EDITION •

BECAUSE MR. OR MS. RIGHT DOES NOT EXIST!

OPRAH WINFREY

TATE PUBLISHING
AND ENTERPRISES, LLC

Mr. or Ms. JUST Right
Copyright © 2016 by Oprah Winfrey. All rights reserved.

No part of this publication may be reproduced, stored in a retrieval system or transmitted in any way by any means, electronic, mechanical, photocopy, recording or otherwise without the prior permission of the author except as provided by USA copyright law.

The opinions expressed by the author are not necessarily those of Tate Publishing, LLC.

Published by Tate Publishing & Enterprises, LLC
127 E. Trade Center Terrace | Mustang, Oklahoma 73064 USA
1.888.361.9473 | www.tatepublishing.com

Tate Publishing is committed to excellence in the publishing industry. The company reflects the philosophy established by the founders, based on Psalm 68:11,
"The Lord gave the word and great was the company of those who published it."

Book design copyright © 2016 by Tate Publishing, LLC. All rights reserved.
Cover design by Niño Carlo Suico
Interior design by Mary Jean Archival

Published in the United States of America

ISBN: 978-1-68207-031-4
1. Family & Relationships / Education
2. Education / Educational Psychology
16.03.02

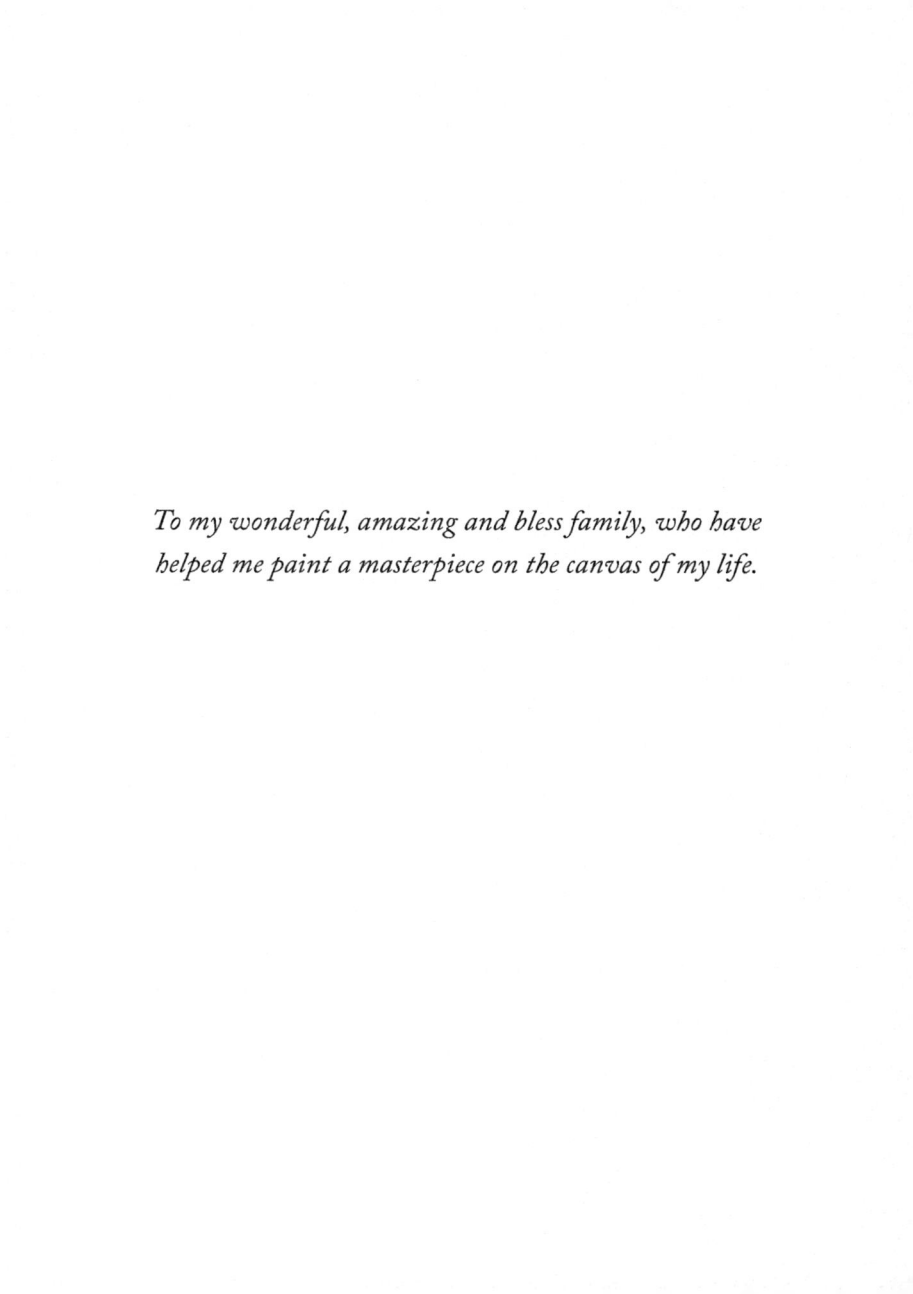

To my wonderful, amazing and bless family, who have helped me paint a masterpiece on the canvas of my life.

CONTENTS

Introduction 11

1	The List	15
2	The Six Steps	29
3	For Women Only!	49
4	For Men Only!	71
5	Art, The Foundation Of True Love	101
6	Case Studies	125

Final Thoughts 145
Glossary 149
Author Bio 153

INTRODUCTION

Generation after generation has wasted countless years searching for something that simply does not exist. We have been tricked by novels, movies, and even the advice of our most trusted friends and family into believing in a fairy tale: the idea that Mr. or Ms. Right is somewhere out there in the world, looking for us.

This sounds beautiful in theory—a man or woman who matches us in every way possible. But we must let go of this delusion. Mr. or Ms. RIGHT is not out there, because he or she **does not exist!**

Every person is unique; each of us has our own distinct interests, ideals, quirks, and habits. The only person who is your perfect match in every way is yourself, because only you know and understand yourself fully. No one else in the world will fit your skin perfectly, because no one else in the world is your mirror image.

Once you understand this basic truth, you are free to accept your true partner: **Mr. or Ms. *JUST* Right**. So stop wasting your precious time on a fantasy that will never come true, and accept the Mr. or Ms. *JUST* Right who might be just around the corner or even standing right in front of you!

> ***Reality Check:*** *This is not a book about fairy tales. If you are in a fairy-tale state of mind, then you need to close this book, put it down, and walk away. The focus of this book is **reality**; it will tell you the truth and nothing but the truth. Much like a polish sausage, the advice will be compact, hearty, and nourishing, but difficult to swallow.*

Out of all the people of different races, faiths, and backgrounds that inhabit the world, your Mr. or Ms. *JUST* Right was created, molded, and shaped perfectly for you. This person will fit you like a hand-tailored suit, fulfilling and satisfying your desires while complementing you in areas of your life that could use improvement. You must remember that Mr. or Ms. *JUST* Right will not be your duplicate! As the old saying goes, "opposites attract!"

There is an **ART** to cultivating relationships with these special mates: **A**ccept the fact that they will fill in the empty gaps in your life like a missing puzzle piece; **R**espect the value that they bring to your life; and **T**rust that you have met your Mr. or Ms. *JUST* Right.

But how will you recognize this person? How will you know which man or woman to accept into your heart? Look no further! If you are ready to embrace the perfect mate, this book will teach you the secret to making the ideal match. *Mr. or Ms.* JUST *Right* is a simple, easy-to-understand guide to choosing, attracting, and having a successful relationship with the *JUST* Right partner.

How-to books and relationship manuals represent 2% of book sales—about $850 million per year. This book differs from the rest because it offers an interactive and perceptive approach that combines common sense with statistical information. Simply put, *Mr. or Ms.* JUST *Right* makes choosing a partner more of a science than a stroke of luck by giving you crucial information:

1. How to determine if someone is your perfect match
2. How to avoid imperfect relationships
3. How to seal the deal with the ideal mate
4. How to maintain the relationship you desire
5. When to exit flawed relationships

This book, which has been described as "a dose of good common sense sprinkled with humor and a pinch of reality," will walk you through the most important journey of your life: finding Mr. or Ms. *JUST* Right.

Author's Note

I am not a licensed psychologist, psychiatrist, or therapist. *Mr. or Ms.* JUST *Right* is not intended to replace psychological counseling or marital therapy. This book offers a relationship philosophy based on my own experiences and those of thousands of people whose relationships I have researched and studied through surveys. The advice is authentic because it is based on the lives and loves of real people, just like you. It will make you think, and it will make you reflect on your life. I hope you enjoy the humor, truth, suspense, and imagination you will find in these pages.

Please note: This book may not be suitable for all audiences; it is recommended for adults eighteen years of age and older.

CHAPTER ONE

THE LIST

HAVE YOU EVER asked yourself why so many people end up in dead-end relationships, dating the wrong people, separating from their spouses, filing for divorce, or moving from one relationship to another—just to repeat the same pattern again and again?

We carefully choose from scores of possible mates and often make a commitment to remain with them throughout our lives. Yet more than forty percent of all marriages end in divorce. On average, first marriages that end in divorce last less than eight years. Why?

Many cite a wide range of factors, including finances, religious beliefs, and sexual compatibility. But the *real explanation* is that most men and women marry

> the **wrong** partner,
> > for the **wrong** reasons,
> > > at the **wrong** time.

Timing is crucial in any relationship. Your first love might have seemed like the perfect mate when you were together. But both of you were probably too young to make a lasting commitment; neither of you knew what you truly wanted. Had you stayed together, your sweetheart would almost certainly be your "Ex."

An ex-lover (as in, "The body is buried under the X of what you once thought you had!") was never your ideal match. Perhaps you were not physically, mentally, or intellectually attracted to this person. Or maybe circumstances, situations, and the weight of the world changed them or even exposed their true, less appealing, selves.

Divorce is second to death as the most traumatic loss that anyone can experience, especially when children are involved. The goal of this book is to help you escape this kind of suffering. So how can you avoid the broken hearts, wasted hours, emotional disappointments, and fractured families? And how can you keep breathing life into the right relationship once you find it?

You must begin by making a list of at least ten adjectives that describe the qualities you seek in a potential mate. You might be lacking—and desire—these characteristics in your own personality, perhaps because you cannot develop them without the help of your ideal partner.

Keep your list of adjectives close to your heart, and review them often. As a relationship progresses, check off the items on your list that your partner possesses. He or she might be smarter than you gave them credit for, or sexier.... Alternately, you might discover that a person you once thought was a deep thinker is merely a bore! If you find someone who meets most (or better yet, all!) of the qualifications on your list, it might be time for you to seal the deal.

In the past, you probably overlooked many appropriate partners because you were too young to appreciate them. Maybe they had squinty eyes or wore the wrong style of shades. You may have even rejected them because you recognized the potential for a long-term relationship and weren't ready for it at the time. But if you are reading this book, you are looking for commitment, and this list is the key to attaining it.

So put your list on the fridge, revisit it often, and revise it as necessary. If you're attracted to someone who does not possess most of these desired qualities, don't waste your time on a relationship that's doomed from the start. Move on.

The Shadow List

Before you start your list, take a long, clear look at yourself in the mirror and examine the qualities you bring to the table. Your "shadow list" might be something like this:

Wonderful,
Thoughtful,
Intelligent,
Healthy,
Wise,
Sexy,
Patient,

Sensible,
Spiritual...
and Available!

You are what you attract, because your attractions are a reflection of yourself. As you create the list that describes your ideal mate, make sure that you can relate to most of the adjectives you choose. If not, then **please stop right now**! You are not in the correct frame of mind to benefit from this list! You cannot expect to fly without wings, or to run if you cannot walk or even crawl. Similarly, you cannot expect to make the perfect match until you have a realistic understanding of yourself and your needs.

Take the time to truly evaluate the qualities that best complement you. Until you find that you can relate to 50 to 60 percent of the words on your mate's list, you should focus on getting to know yourself a little better.

Some Simple Math

If you have completely fulfilled certain qualities, you don't need to include these traits on your mate's list! Your partner should help you round out the areas of your life that you would like to improve. If you have already developed a quality fully, take it off of your partner's list; you do not need his or her assistance with it. Your cup is full—you don't want it to spill over!

For instance, if you have reached 100 percent of your desired level of spirituality, you should not actively seek a partner who has also reached 100 percent spirituality. You have both maximized this trait; combining your experiences will not magically result in 200 percent fulfillment in this area of your life!

Imagine, instead, that you have attained 50 to 60 percent of the spiritual growth you seek, and want to fill the remaining emptiness. Your best bet is to invite a partner into your life who will help you attain 100 percent spiritual fulfillment. This partner's level should be at least 40 to 50 percent, so that together you can balance one another and reach a complete score of 100 percent.

Keep in mind that some qualities cannot be fulfilled through other people's assistance. Knowing oneself fully will allow you to understand what you are seeking and what you can hope to attain from a relationship.

A True Partnership

It has been proven that couples build stronger bonds when both parties maintain their full independence. Clinging to expectations and becoming dependent on your mate will do little to help your relationship.

Most people find it difficult when things don't go quite the way they thought they should. While it's natural to have your own preferences, anger over unfulfilled expectations is one of the major hindrances to most relationships. I would estimate that these conflicts—might be over other important things like finances or minor things like behavioral traits—destroy at least ninety percent of potentially successful relationships.

For instance, assuming you don't need his physical assistance, there is no reason to throw a fuss if your date doesn't open the car door for you. Do not let your expectations of certain behavior ruin your night—or your relationship. Simply open your own door and gracefully enter the car.

Perhaps you are upset because your partner opened doors for you in the early stages of the relationship, but stopped at some point without any explanations. One of the biggest mistakes people tend to make when they enter into a new relationship is to wear a "disguise suit"—in other words, to pretend to be someone they are not. As time progresses, these suits inevitably come off. Without them, the couple might not be compatible. If you build a relationship on a foundation of deceit, how long can it possibly last? When you become involved with someone, you must show not only your best self, but also your true self.

In addition, you must continue to be as independent as life allows. For instance, if you're out on a date at the movies and your mate has purchased the movie tickets, you should buy the popcorn. Or if your mate pays for dinner, you should leave the tip—and make it a good one! Don't limit yourself or prevent yourself from doing things that could improve the relationship. Never hold yourself back because you believe your partner will, might, or should do something for you.

The word "partner," after all, implies a high amount of teamwork. In team sports, the players rely on one another to carry their own weight. Of course, not all players have the same physical or mental abilities. The stronger or more alert players are usually the ones who come up with the master plan that successfully carries the team to the finish line. Make sure you choose a partner with the strength and independence to be a valuable part of your team.

If your mate changes for the better during the course of the relationship, be grateful for it and continue to perform at your best. But if your mate begins paying too little attention to areas that he or she can control, then you have to make a decision about remaining with this person. Remember, nobody wants to be taken advantage of or abused by someone else, and it's highly unlikely that a relationship will thrive when one of the parties feels that way.

So let's revisit the issue of opening the car door. A woman might be fully independent in all areas of life before she meets a man, but still make the mistake of beginning to surrender her independence to him on the first date. She should open her own car door, especially if she is also a driver! If she doesn't have a physical infirmity, why should she rely on her date for a simple physical task? If he insists on opening the door to impress her, she should accept his generosity with a warning: *Don't pretend to be someone you are not.* If he knows he'll stop opening doors for her one day, he should simply begin as he means to continue.

When partners maintain their independence, it is easier for the relationship to remain balanced. You must never lose yourself, and you must never try to change your partner. That is a surefire way to build an unstable relationship based on half-truths. Use your time wisely and stay in tune with yourself. Always remember who you are and what you want. Don't forget the reasons why you allowed your partner into your life, and don't lose your own path to your own future.

Look Carefully!

Remember, there are many, many fish in the dating "pond." If you catch one that you know will not satisfy your desires for whatever reason, throw it back and keep fishing. Your list—which should be on your refrigerator!—will help you choose the right "fish."

> ***Celebrity Example:*** *Jennifer Lopez has no problem throwing back the dissatisfying fish that she brings home—over and over and over again! She knows she's worthy of the right relationship, and she will keep fishing until she finds it. For more on Ms. Lopez, turn to Chapter Six, which provides an in-depth case study of her relationships.*

To catch the fish you desire, you must be patient, pay attention, stay consistent, and refuse to settle for just any kind of fish. If you do accept an inferior catch, you will be returning to the pond sooner than you'd like, because you still have to fulfill the needs that the fish you took home did not meet.

Choose the location of your search wisely; you need to be in the right place at the right time to find the mate you desire. Fish live in the water, not on jagged rocks. You aren't a hunter stalking a lion—you are a fisherman (or fisherwoman!) looking for a catch to take home with you. If you are ready to meet your Mr. or Ms. *JUST* Right, you'll have a hard time finding that special person in the jagged rocks of a nightclub or a strip bar. I'd put your chances right up there with winning the lottery.

> ***Reality Check:*** *Life is not a fairytale, and we cannot think about love in fairytale terms. Let's keep it real. A married man who pursues a single woman, for instance, cannot give her all of the attention she desires, especially when he has a family that awaits him at home. And how*

often does an intelligent, spiritual, wise man go to Sunset Boulevard to choose a bride?

Unless you are willing to **accept** your mate's lifestyle, **respect** his or her decisions, and have full **trust** in your partner, you are in for a very rocky road. Developing **A**cceptance, **R**espect, and **T**rust (**ART**) is the key to a promising future in any relationship because ART is the foundation of an enduring love. No couple can survive without this blueprint for success. We'll discuss ART in greater detail in Chapter Five.

Learning to Negotiate: The TWO for ONE Rule

Negotiation is the best form of therapy for every relationship, particularly in its darkest moments. The "TWO for ONE Rule" is the most important facet of negotiation. Couples that obey this rule tend to have greater balance in their relationships and treat one another with greater fairness. It helps both parties take each other's feelings into consideration, and it allows the partner who is making the request to think twice before reacting to or judging the other partner's flaws.

The TWO for ONE Rule states that the person who is asking for something should be willing to sacrifice TWO things for every ONE thing that he or she wants the other partner to alter. Keep in mind that no one is perfect; before you try to point out the specks of dirt in someone else's eye, you should take a good look in the mirror and make sure your own eyes are clean.

Take your time and have fun with the negotiations in your relationship. Just be sure to complete each agreed-upon set of adjustments before starting up a new round of bargaining!

The Debby James Story

I'm Debby James, a thirty-six-year-old attorney who resides in the Bay Area of San Francisco with my husband and our two lovely kids. When the ideas in this book were introduced to me two years ago, the "TWO for ONE Rule" saved my marriage of six years.

During my childhood, education, and career, I adopted many habits that I brought with me into my marriage. My husband did the same. When we began living together, it was difficult for us to reach an agreement about which of these habits should make their way into our home. This led to a lot of tension!

For instance, my husband disliked it if I answered my work cell phone when I was at home. And while I didn't think twice about loudly popping my chewing gum in our house, he found the sound very aggravating. My greatest source of annoyance was his smoking. I found the habit disgusting, and spent years complaining about the smell of smoke and the risk of cancer it brought into our home.

During all of this nagging, I never stopped to ask myself if my behavior was contributing to his smoking habits. When I complained about the cigarettes, he would often reply that he found my habit of loudly popping my gum just as annoying, but I refused to listen. I didn't think anything was wrong with popping gum—I thought he was just complaining about it to get back at me for nagging him about his smoking. But I now know that the sound truly grated on his nerves, raising his anxiety levels to the point where he really needed a cigarette!

A trusted friend of mine recommended that I read this book, and it saved our marriage. I immediately recognized the source of our problem. Going back down memory lane, I thought about our first date. I remembered opening a pack of chewing gum after dinner and placing a piece in my mouth. Not long after I started chewing (and most likely popping!) the gum, he pulled over at a gas station to buy a pack of cigarettes.

I realized with shock that my own habit had intensified his! Over the years, I had refused to acknowledge that the things he found annoying in me were causing him so much stress that he needed the relief of smoking. In relationships, we often upset the people we care about the most without even realizing it. When I read about the "TWO for ONE Rule," I immediately knew what needed to be done.

My husband and I sat down together to talk about the rule, and we decided to try it. I began the negotiation by requesting that he stop smoking; he immediately asked that I stop popping my gum. His second request caught me by surprise: he mentioned that I should limit the amount of guests I invited to our house. My family and friends visited us two or three times per week, and I never knew that this frequency bothered him!

Was I upset? Of course! My family is everything to me, and I was reluctant to limit my time with them. But I reminded myself that he had left his own family to start a new one with our children and me. I had to accept and respect his desire to end his day in relative peace, in the company of just his wife and kids.

It's been sixteen months since we negotiated our agreement, and everything has changed. I could care less about chewing gum now, because my dentist has pointed out that my teeth are in so much better shape since I quit. My husband is 100% nicotine free and we now have clean air in our home. When I want to visit my friends and family, I just go to their houses. And I love dropping the kids off with them and coming home to spend quality time with my husband. This book has brought peace to my home, balance to my family, and health to my marriage, my lungs, and my teeth!"

Debby James, P.A.

So what can we learn from Debby's story? To have a successful relationship, we need to be aware of our own strengths and weaknesses and how they impact our partners. When we reach this understanding, we can negotiate adjustments that will strengthen the bonds we have with our mates—and even save a relationship.

CHAPTER TWO

THE SIX STEPS

It's very common to feel confused about how to find the right mate. While dating might come naturally to you, the process of selecting the person you will accept fully into your life can be tricky. This chapter breaks that journey down into six steps:

1. Know Where NOT to Go
2. Know Where to Go
3. Look in the Mirror
4. Find Your Age Group
5. Match Your Personality Types
6. Use the ART Canvas

Now let's put these steps to work!

STEP 1: Know Where NOT to Go

The reason most sexual affairs don't last is because all types of relationships need work and compromise. Sex usually multiplies both the benefits and the pitfalls of being part of a couple, because it places the emphasis on connecting physically instead of emotionally. While fulfilling our sexual needs can help us lead longer, happier, and even healthier lives, we have to look beyond the physical when choosing a mate.

You must understand what makes a relationship work before you can have a successful one. We often bring unrealistic expectations into our unions, which leads to heartache. This pain can be avoided by examining the misinformation that has shaped our unworkable expectations. We receive this information from many sources: parents, peers, society, television, movies, our own egos, and (particularly for men) their sexual desires. Should you trust the messages you receive from love songs, soap operas, and romance novels? From Disney movies? From *Cosmopolitan* magazine or *Maxim*?

Don't Go to the Media!

We're constantly being bombarded with misleading images and body types, both in print and on the screen. At best, these ideals are something to move toward; at worst, they plant unrealistic ideas about people and situations in our subconscious minds. When we were children and watched cartoons, we knew the cat on the screen was not a real cat. We have to put the media we view today in that same framework. It simply isn't based in reality.

Don't Go to Friends and Associates!

You definitely don't want to rely upon everything your friends tell you. They have their own backgrounds and angles, and they're likely as confused as you are. They may also give you opinions that are not based on reality. For instance, a friend might not want to hurt your feelings by telling you the truth, or a false friend could simply be jealous of you and refuse to lead you in the right direction.

Be Careful with Advice from Your Parents!

I suppose perfect parents might exist, but odds are good yours aren't completely infallible! Take what your family—particularly your parents—tells you with a grain of salt. Yes, they love you and want you to be happy, but they don't always know what's right for your situation.

Guidelines from parents are often extremely fractured and confusing. Parents raise sons and daughters, not husbands and wives; they probably can't view you objectively as a potential mate. And older generations might be outdated in their thinking and give information based on the experiences of their youth.

Today, fewer couples are choosing marriage, and if they do, they are leaving their spouses more often and more quickly...

with no consequences. Divorce has lost its social stigma. Society sees and accepts failed relationships as normal, and the single parent as a kind of folk hero. Over sixty percent of U.S. divorces are "uncontested": the two parties come to an agreement without having a hearing about their property, their children, or support issues.

One of your life's biggest decisions, time commitments, emotional and financial investments—and poof! It has vanished, often leaving behind nothing but pain and wasted years.

Life is short, and you're up at bat only a few times. You've got to hit a home run. And you've never played this particular game before, since no relationship is the same. Every relationship is a unique journey of two individuals meeting the future together.

So don't base your decisions on unrealistic ideas of romance or biased opinions. You must learn where to go for useful information.

STEP 2: Know Where to Go

There are three basic kinds of knowledge:

- **Prior Knowledge:** Based completely on one's own experiences
- **Accepted Knowledge**: Reasonable beliefs one has learned (Example: Even though you may not have visited the state of Montana, you know it exists)

- **Borrowed Knowledge**: Based on the experiences of someone we know personally (Example: You know about the army because your cousin was in it)

Which kind of knowledge can we use to sort through this mating mess? We'll examine each of them below, but I'll give you a hint: it starts with "Borrowed!"

Prior Knowledge

Prior knowledge is limited, impatient, fickle, and sometimes self-destructive. It can't be relied upon.

> *Reality Check: This is especially true for men, who often think with two heads! Even if men could rely on their own experiences, they have limited time to fill their knowledge bank in this manner, since they have so many relationships available to them. As they say in New Zealand, "So many sheep, so little time!"*

Relationships and their emotional turmoil can be exhausting, leaving you with a warped view of choosing a mate. In addition, you can't get enough samples to have an adequate perspective on what you're going through, which makes you an even less trustworthy resource for yourself.

We all have a mischievous devil on our shoulders that delights in ruining relationships: the self-destruct mechanism. Our own fear and sense of confusion can destroy a promising connection.

And then there's the turn-off switch. What we once liked, we now detest—seemingly overnight! For example, a woman might initially be attracted to aggression and flattery, but later see the same qualities as control issues and manipulation. Perhaps the humorous person you were initially attracted to is now the silly person who takes nothing seriously. Or the seriousness you once appreciated is now bringing you down.

Of course, there's always a tendency to project onto and blame our partners for faults that may be our own. The mind works in unusual ways, and not always in our favor.

Does this thought pattern sound familiar? *"I fell in love with someone like this before and I messed it up, but it will be different this time!"* No, it won't. Making the same mistakes and hoping for different outcomes is the definition of insanity.

You're probably familiar with the story of Rihanna and Chris Brown. These talented singers and actors recently made the headlines for more than just their talents. They became the poster children for dysfunctional relationships. In 2009, Chris Brown was convicted of a felony for assaulting Rihanna during an argument. Photos of her battered face quickly made their way around the Internet, and the public rallied behind Rihanna as a victim of domestic abuse.

To everyone's shock, the couple started seeing one another again in 2012. Rihanna told the public, "He's not the monster everybody thinks. He's a good person." She claimed that he had changed. In other words, she decided to make the same mistake again and hope for a different outcome. Insanity! The lack of Acceptance, Respect, and Trust (ART) in this relationship makes it very unlikely that it will last.

Don't repeat Rihanna's mistakes. You might be in denial if you hear yourself saying things like:

> *I know it's not right, but I love him…*
> *None of my friends like her, but…*
> *No one is giving him a fair chance…*
> *We always get along when we're alone…*
> *She'd treat me better if only I would…*

Love may be blind, but deliberately closing your eyes doesn't create love. It's natural to want to please someone who gives you romantic attention. Just understand that you can't base all of your knowledge on your prior experiences, especially if it seems like you aren't learning from your mistakes.

Accepted Knowledge

Accepted knowledge misses the point. It doesn't allow for the textured individual—the unique sensual, biological, emotional, and psychological complexities of your situation. These nuances are what make up your life, and accepted knowledge takes none of them into consideration.

This type of knowledge is particularly problematic when it comes to dating and sex, both of which rely on experimentation and personal growth. You can gain much from reading or hearing about someone else's experiences, but no two people are the same. Imagine asking a deaf person to read a page of sheet music and tell you how she thinks it might sound. The ideas she comes up with may be beautiful, but they are unlikely to be accurate. In the same way, you can't fully rely on others' ideas about relationships and sexuality.

It's impossible to jam a romance into a box, expecting it to fit neatly and turn out exactly as you think it should. People can—and generally will—surprise you. A mate might seem to be perfect according to society's views, but he or she might be completely wrong for you.

You should also beware of axioms or jokes that make light of relationships:

- *"A woman needs a man like a pond fish needs sunlight."* We are not meant to live our lives alone. Our drive to come together is why the human race is expanding and will continue to expand.
- *"I haven't spoken to my wife in years—I didn't want to interrupt her."* In a true partnership, both parties listen to and respect one another's opinions.
- *"Marriage is a three-ring circus: engagement ring, wedding ring, and suffering."* A strong marriage is a source of joy and comfort for both parties.

Conventional "wisdom" like this may be good material for stand-up comedians, but don't let it affect your opinions about relationships or the other sex. When you accept your Mr. or Ms. *JUST* Right into your life, you'll realize how foolish these generalizations are.

And so we're left with one kind of knowledge…

Borrowed Knowledge

Use great care and discretion when dealing with borrowed knowledge, which is like a finger pointing to the moon. It's not the moon. It's not the journey. What you do with your journey is the quilt of your life. In the end, that is where wisdom lies.

The most reliable form of borrowed knowledge comes from someone you know, trust, and admire, and who has already found what you are seeking. You wouldn't ask a poor man how to make money, or an overweight man how to build stomach muscles! So why would you ask someone who isn't in a strong relationship for information about dating?

The challenge is finding that model. Examine the lives of your close friends and family members. If you can envision yourself living as they do, chances are good they would make a good teacher. The pages of this book also offer a lot of borrowed knowledge about your age and the power you hold, about discovering your personality and passions, and about finding ways to keep your relationship alive and exciting. Use it well.

You can, and should, look to other places for borrowed knowledge. Group interactions head the list. Watch how people behave toward one another and build conclusions based on your observations. Does your best friend's marriage seem to be thriving? If so, what brought them together and what keeps them so strong? This is very different from relying on the opinions of others. Here, you are learning through observation, studying the patterns that work for others and avoiding the mistakes that some are making.

The next step is applying these lessons to your life. As Confucius remarked, "It's easier to find a ready teacher than a ready student." In other words, there is plenty of good information out there. The responsibility to learn from it is yours. And your prospective match, like you, must have the will to make it work.

The *JUST* Right person is out there. No, the process of finding your true mate is not simple. No, the journey is not without hills and valleys. Mr. or Ms. *JUST* Right will not be without flaws. But you can maximize your odds of success by using the correct kind of information. This book will teach you how to focus on age-appropriate candidates with suitable personality types and similar goals and interests.

STEP 3: Look in the Mirror

Before you can accept your ideal mate, you must come to a clear understanding of who you are. All of us are a mix of our genetics, choices, parenting, experience, and environment. No one is the same at forty-eight as they were at eighteen, just as no two eighteen-year-olds are the same. *If you don't know who you are, finding the moon to your sun is impossible.*

It's essential that you know exactly what you have to offer and exactly what your potential mate desires. Read carefully what your target Age Group (see Step 4, below) expects from your Age Group. Chapters Three and Four will give you in-depth information about these expectations. For now, let's start with a simple example: women between the ages of 18 and 25 expect a man who is 36 or older to offer financial security.

> ***Reality Check:*** *Don't try to fool yourself. Living in denial is an excellent way to derail your love life. If you're thirty-six years old, but feel twenty-five… you're still thirty-six. If you're a mature eighteen-year-old who feels like you're in your twenties… you're still eighteen.*
>
> *You don't want to be like Blanche Devereaux from the television show "The Golden Girls." No one took Blanche, an older woman pretending to be a young southern belle, seriously because her behavior was ridiculous. And men, you don't want to be the old guy at the bar who is pretending to be a charming young prince.*

Be honest about what you bring to the table, because the truth will come out in the end. If you're broke, you're broke—faking it until you make it rarely works. You still have plenty to offer even if you lack certain attributes; you just might have to extend your age group and make some compromises.

Remember, the *JUST* Right person for you is looking for one thing: you! He or she wants exactly what you have, and will not be put off by what you don't have. But to find this person, you have to understand exactly who you are.

STEP 4: Find Your Age Group

Appraising Where the Power Lies

Age is far more than just a number. Comparing your Age Group to your partner's Age Group will help you determine where the power lies in your relationship. This power can shift, be wasted, or be abused; but knowing who has the power enables you to predict behavior, control the situation, and spare yourself countless hours wasted on relationships that are going nowhere.

THE AGE GROUPS CHART:

WOMEN:

AGE	IDENTITY	POSITION IN THE POWER PLAY
18–25	*"Innocence"*	She has many choices and can choose who she wants.
26–35	*"In Denial"*	She settles, or accepts whoever selects her. She's often intimidating.
36–older	*"Whatever!"*	She wants companionship and predictability. Almost anyone will do.

MEN:

AGE	IDENTITY	POSITION IN THE POWER PLAY
18–25	*"Experimenting"*	He will accept almost anyone who chooses him.
26–35	*"The Catch"*	He gets who he chooses, and is at peak mental strength.
36–older	*"Oh Snap!"*	He depends on his assets and his power to get the person he wants.

Aiming at the correct Age Group will save you an astonishing amount of time and energy. When you cross-reference the Age Group(s) you have chosen, you will be able to see what *they're* looking for. But most importantly, you will understand who has the power and whether the relationship has a chance of survival.

As you consider these Age Groups, keep in mind that the best relationships develop when both parties are able to choose each other—in other words, each of them has the power of choosing his or her mate at some point in the relationship. If that is not possible, it is generally preferable for the man to choose the woman. When the woman chooses the man, he can feel emasculated, which frequently damages the relationship.

The Good News

People are constantly moving in and out of Age Groups. Partners in different groups sometimes qualify for each other at different times in their lives. That high school sweetheart might be perfect for you by your thirty-year reunion. That gawky teenager you met ten years ago might have stepped into his or her full power and become a great choice. You need to take the long-range view.

The guidelines provided in this book will enable you to understand the dynamics of male–female interactions and choose

> the **right** partner,
> > for the **right** reasons,
> > > at the **right** time.

They will be your blueprints to building a smooth, loving relationship. Chapter Three (For Women Only!) and Chapter

Four (For Men Only!) will teach you everything you need to know about Age Groups and show you exactly how to use your knowledge to make the ideal match.

STEP 5: Match Your Personality Types

Twenty-five hundred years ago, the Greeks identified seven different character types. You should try to determine which category best defines both you and your partner. Identifying your personality types will help establish how the two of you will relate to one another and whether you can reside comfortably together. Chickens and cats can't live together in a chicken coop, nor can a lion be trained to be a house pet. Similarly, clashing personality types will have great difficulty building a peaceful, fulfilling life together.

The Classic Personality Types:

1. **Guardian**: Dedicated to protecting others
2. **Artist**: Loves beauty and is often whimsical
3. **Idealist**: Clings to firm beliefs
4. **Rationalist**: Uses logic and reason as a guide
5. **Melancholic**: Tends to be withdrawn or moody
6. **Fearful**: Approaches life with caution
7. **Sickly**: Struggles with health and lack of energy
8. **Damaged**: Trying to overcome past traumas

OPRAH WINFREY

Begin by gauging who you are. Which of these categories best defines how you approach life and love? The Personality Type Chart (below) will help you figure it out.

Calculating Your Personality Type

The charts in this section will allow you to identify both your own personality type and your partner's personality type. Calculate your scores in each category, and then calculate your partner's scores in each category. The categories in which you have the highest scores are your strongest personality types.

Your Personality Type Chart

Personality Type	How Strongly You Identify with This Personality Type				
	Always (4 Points)	Often (3 Points)	Sometimes (2 points)	Rarely (1 points)	Never (0 points)
Guardian					
Artist					
Idealist					
Rationalist					
Melancholic					
Fearful					
Sickly					
Damaged					
Total Score:					

Your Partner's Personality Type Chart

Personality Type	How Strongly You Identify with This Personality Type				
	Always (4 Points)	Often (3 Points)	Sometimes (2 points)	Rarely (1 points)	Never (0 points)
Guardian					
Artist					
Idealist					
Rationalist					
Melancholic					
Fearful					
Sickly					
Damaged					
Total Score:					

(Likert scale, Christian Vanek 2012).

Now, take a look at the categories where you scored the highest, and where your partner scored the highest. These are your strongest personality types. Write them down below:

Your personality type:

_____

Your partner's personality type:

_____

You may find that you score highly in two or more categories. Perhaps you are an Idealistic Guardian or a Melancholic Rationalist. But focus on pinpointing the motivations that drive you most often, and choose just **one** personality type for yourself and just **one** for your partner. Hint: Your true personality type was probably the first one you identified with when you were reading the list of categories.

Now that you know your personality type, you can determine how well you and your partner fit together. The goal is to find a pairing that is balanced.

Partners who share the same personality type might be attracted to one another at first, but that initial attraction is less likely to last. Two melancholy people, for instance, will not give each other the balance that a good relationship should have. If you and your partner end up with two or more of the same scores based on the personality chart, this is a sign that you should rethink the relationship.

On the other hand, pairings that clash with one another should be avoided. A dreamy artist who seeks beauty in life is unlikely to find happiness with a melancholy person who approaches the world with a pessimistic attitude. Your personality types should complement one another, not clash with one another.

STEP 6: Use the ART (Acceptance, Respect, and Trust) Model

The ART model is so important that it truly needs a chapter of its own—we can't fully cover it in a short section. So we will return to it after spending more time discovering what we need to seek in a partner. If you're anxious to get started on this step, you can find it in Chapter Five!

CHAPTER THREE

FOR WOMEN ONLY!

When it comes to age, women are in a very different situation than men: the clock is constantly ticking toward the time when childbearing is no longer possible. The main questions a woman must consider are:

1. What do you want? Do you want to be cherished, wasted, or left alone?
2. What's the best way to go about getting it?
3. Do you want children? If so, how many and when?
4. Where does your career fit into your plans?

If the answer is "no" to children, your timetable for marriage is much the same as a man's.

If the answer is "yes" or "maybe," you have roughly ten years to choose the right man, make a good marriage, have some time together as a couple, and conceive a child. By the age of 28, women begin having trouble becoming pregnant. By 35, conception without fertility treatment is difficult. By 40, your chances might be negligible.

Women need to recognize the age at which they have their full power as quickly as possible. They must then learn to embrace it, enjoy it, and use it appropriately to attain their desires. Women also need to know when the power in a relationship belongs to the man, and to learn to embrace and enjoy their own role.

The most important, difficult, and exciting decision in your life is who to accept as the father of your children. But many women make a grave mistake when they decide that they're ready to get married: they simply accept the man they are currently with. Most women have deep-seated maternal instincts that make them believe they can take an adequate male and nurture him, molding him into a great mate. This is highly unlikely; by the time men are of marriageable age, their personalities have already taken root. With men, you get what you see—or even less. Sometimes much less. Don't delude yourself.

Women face another unique challenge that men don't have to consider. They must take great care in reacting to the sexual cues of men. Men are highly sexual creatures, and can sometimes read more into our behavior than we actually mean. Avoiding the wrong situation is so much easier than removing oneself from it.

Women can also change more quickly than men. They tend to be the first see that a relationship is coming to an end. A graceful exit technique is very important here, because an annoyingly high percentage of men have trouble with rejection. Some might even become obsessive and obnoxious about it. It is better to get to know a man well than to move too quickly with him, thereby exposing yourself to the risk of unpleasant surprises.

Finally, the sad reality is that there are more good women out there than good men. Women are simply wired differently; most want to be in a committed relationship and raise children in a happy home. Men are biologically driven to "play the field." It's harsh, but it's true.

So women, find out who you are and where you stand, and **take advantage of your power while you have it**!

AGE GROUPS CHART

WOMEN:

AGE	IDENTITY	POSITION IN THE POWER PLAY
18–25	"Innocence"	She has many choices and can choose who she wants.
26–35	"In Denial"	She settles, or accepts whoever selects her. She's often intimidating.
36–older	"Whatever!"	She wants companionship and predictability. Almost anyone will do.

Let's take a closer look at what this all means, and how it impacts your relationships with men in varying Age Groups.

Women Aged 18–25: *"Innocence"*

When a woman is between the ages of 18 and 25, she's at the peak of her beauty, fertility, and vitality. She is also a bit naïve. Most importantly, she has the full power to choose almost any man she wants. Her *innocence*, openness, and happiness are very attractive to the men she meets. Young men want her because young men want anyone! "*The Catch*" wants her for a fun relationship and possibly marriage. Older men want her as a trophy to display.

Innocence may be bliss, but there's no bliss in letting your power slip through your fingers! Use your time in this Age Group wisely to discover what you want in a mate and build a strong relationship.

"Innocence"—Should You Get Involved with a Man Aged 18–25?

If you do, he should damned well have something to offer! He should be caring, gentle, and patient. He should be a good listener, and he should genuinely like you.

Don't be just a "score." While a woman in this Age Group is naturally innocent, she shouldn't make stupid choices. Men of this age are not looking for a permanent relationship. If

MR. OR MS. JUST RIGHT

they rush you into sex, tell them to take a hike! While we're on that subject, make sure you take control of all decisions involving birth control. The responsibility for a pregnancy will lie on you; do not allow your partner to make foolish choices that will change the course of your life.

While it is possible that a younger man will become your life partner, a man in this Age Group is generally *experimenting*, finding himself, and unsure of exactly what he wants. These are bad, bad, *bad* qualities for a mate. He may even have other women in his life. Don't try to make it something it's not. You might be ready for marriage, but is he?

Even if he's truly interested in marriage, men of his age are often financially unstable. The leading cause of divorce is financial conflict, and you don't want to help that statistic grow. Make sure you know what you're getting into before you commit.

If a woman of this Age Group dates a man of the same Age Group, things might change dramatically when he reaches the second age bracket (26–35). He might realize that he didn't choose her—that she, in fact, chose him—which could create control issues (See Chapter Four for more information on control issues with "*The Catch*"). This could eventually destroy the relationship. He may leave her or even cheat on her because he would rather be with a woman he has chosen. If that happens, the woman will have wasted some of her most valuable months or years on him, and he'll be merrily on his way, enjoying his new life as "*The Catch*."

A woman between the ages of 18 and 25 who is ready to settle down or find Mr. *JUST* Right will do best by dating men between the ages of 26 and 35. These men are the most likely to offer a serious commitment. These two Age Groups are at their full power; when they merge, the strength of their relationship reflects that power.

So enjoy yourself, explore your needs, insist on protection (and gifts on occasion!), and take advantage of your youth. Educate yourself well—this is a great time to discover art, music, and poetry—and use your bliss wisely. You can even date that guy with tattoos on his head, or that sax player in an unknown band. Just be aware that the years are passing, and your time of power will come to an end soon.

"Innocence"—Should You Get Involved with a Man Aged 26–35?

In many ways, this is the ideal combination for your Age Groups. Men of this age are often financially secure and ready to settle down. They're drawn to your youth, your fertility, and your *innocence*. It's a perfect fit!

In this dynamic, both parties have the power, but if she looks carefully, stays a step ahead of him, and makes wise decisions, "The *Innocent*" can catch "*The Catch*." It's important to make sure the man believes he is choosing you. Men don't want to be "trapped" by women; they want to feel in control, and to pursue and win a desirable partner. When you know

MR. OR MS. JUST RIGHT

he's in the right frame of mind, you can decide whether or not you will accept him as a mate.

Choosing a spouse is possibly the most important decision of your life. Choose wisely, and don't draw silly generalizations. Don't blow off a good man because you like taller guys, or you think he is too quiet. And don't hold yourself back because you think you're too young to settle down. You might feel young, but your body is growing older every day. If you know you want children, these years of your life are the real deal, and "*The Catch*" is your best bet.

"*Innocence*"—*Should You Get Involved with a Man Aged 36 or Older?*

There are two excellent reasons to pair up with a man over the age of 36: money and security. If a young woman chooses an older man, he'd better be offering her the easy life! She should have a clear and honest understanding of what her decision will entail. For men this age, power lies within the possession of their assets. Most retired postal workers are not in a position to choose "The Innocent." Movie stars with mansions, on the other hand, have their pick of the young ladies, no matter what their age. Think of the late Anna Nicole Smith and her far, *far* older husband—who just so happened to be astonishingly wealthy!

Men are virile to the grave, so fertility doesn't have to be a consideration, barring a physical incapacity. But make sure you know his position on having children and how he wants them to be reared. Older men may not be interested in bringing rambunctious kids into their lives, or they may have old-fashioned opinions on raising them that don't match your own views. Make sure you are on the same page.

Of course, this pairing has its own challenges. Men of this age are generally set in their ways, which might be frustrating to an independent woman. Hopefully, their appreciation of their good luck in finding a young bride will offset this issue.

> ***Reality Check:*** *If a man is more than fifteen years your senior, there will be generational differences to take into consideration. He might like different music, have older friends, and live life at a different pace. These factors should not automatically eliminate him from the running; they could lead you to enjoy things you otherwise wouldn't have been exposed to. However, the generational differences might be so profound that they detract significantly from his potential as Mr. JUST Right.*

Older men can be a wonderful answer to your search for a partner. They have sowed their wild oats; they have their lives in the order that they will likely remain; they know what they want. They can be most generous and might limit the demands they make on their partners. They are also more likely to appreciate a young woman. Should they have their health and their finances in good shape and fulfill your desires in a mate, they need to be considered as an option.

It may not be a Hollywood ending, but it may be the right ending for you. Remember, this isn't a fairy tale, so let go of your fairy-tale notions.

Women Aged 26–35: "*In Denial*"

Between the ages of 26 and 35, women are in the denial period. I know you're saying, "Not me!" right now—that's the definition of denial! You are in denial about being *In Denial*, and you need to face reality before your misperceptions damage your relationships and your chances of finding Mr. *JUST* Right.

If you hear yourself quoting Beyoncé's "Irreplaceable" ("I can have another you in a minute!") or if you find yourself declaring that you are in control of a relationship when you know, deep down, that you really aren't, then you are in for a treat when reality comes crashing down around you. You're kidding yourself, and it's not doing you any favors.

Most women in this Age Group think that they still have the full power to get whoever and whatever they want. They base this belief on the fact that a woman between the ages of 26 and 35 generally has her act together, has finished school, has a job, is comfortable with her body, and knows what she wants. This sounds like good reasoning, but it isn't the way the world works, and this attitude can be a stumbling block for "*In Denial.*"

A woman of this age, with her extensive achievements, can easily appear intimidating to most of the men that she finds attractive. The men know that she no longer wants to accept just anybody and her attitude toward dating has shifted. In other words, they understand that she is ready to settle down and is looking for a similar level of accomplishments in a mate.

To overcome this problem, you must realize that you no longer have the power to choose the man. Remember, most women of this age will eventually accept or settle for a partner for a number of very common reasons: "He's a little shorter than my type, but he treats me well" or "He's not that cute, but he's nice to my kids." I'm sure you've heard this kind of thought process from many women in the 26–35 Age Group. Pay attention to what women your age are doing—this is the kind of borrowed knowledge that will enable you to understand your current role in the dating game. You are no longer the chooser, but are now accepting a man's choice for the reasons that are right for you.

How does this affect your relationship with other Age Groups? As we will discuss below, younger men will date you because they'll date anybody, men your age are the choosers and you'll have to accept their decisions, and older men might meet you as an equal—maybe you'll choose each other.

However...

Younger men are likely to be a waste of time. All available women desire men of your Age Group. And older men might be more interested in older women, who have had more time to master seduction and manipulation.

You can look good. You can have everything going for you. You can put yourself out there as a desirable partner. But you have to face the facts. You can lead a man to water, but you can't make him tap dance.

"In Denial"—Should You Get Involved with a Man Aged 18–25?

If a woman between the ages of 26 and 35 is dating a man in the 18–25 Age Group, it usually means that she is lonely and is looking for companionship and sex. This pairing generally will not last.

Woman mature faster and have a different timeline than a younger man (remember, that biological clock is ticking!). Younger men are interested in exploring their options and proving that they're strong and virile. If you condone their immature behavior or try to go along with them for the ride, you're fooling yourself. You'll just end up wasting more of your time.

Young men want to map out their own futures; unless they are looking for a mother figure, they don't want to be a mini-you, and they don't want you to baby them. At the same time, they won't be much help with your own needs, since you have more experience and wisdom than they possess. And we all have needs—otherwise, we wouldn't need a partner at all.

Simply put, it's not going to work out. You know it, and he knows it. It's ok to have some fun, but don't commit too much time to the party, and don't let your heart get broken.

The sole advantage of dating a young man is that he will eventually become "*The Catch.*" If you are patient with him and if he feels like you complete him, he might choose you when he reaches that stage.

"In Denial"—Should You Get Involved with a Man Aged 26–35?

This is your best match, but it is also the most difficult for you to attain. By this point in your life, you've probably had sexual encounters, had long-term relationships, and even been in love. The time of the Princess and the White Knight is in the distant past. You should be enjoying yourself while staying grounded in reality.

Remember that "*The Catch*" is called that for a reason. Men of this age have the power and are genetically inclined to use it. Currently, the average age at marriage in the U.S. is 26.8 years for men and 25.1 years for women. Your time for choosing is up.

The good news is that women are genetically inclined to be one step ahead of men! It's time to be clever. So surround yourself with eligible men. Make sure you always look good. Always be ready to be chosen, because dating a man in this Age Group is like fishing: things happen when they happen.

MR. OR MS. JUST RIGHT

If *"In Denial"* wants to raise a family, she faces a serious complication: the very limited numbers of years remaining for her to find a mate, marry, and have children. Focusing on marriage and family is in your best interests at this age, but there are still many factors to consider.

Divorce is so common today that family-minded women need to weigh the chances of a relationship's success. You should give preference to men from similar backgrounds and religions, because large disparities in experiences and beliefs can lead to tension in a marriage. While he's just enjoying being with you, you have to do the hard part: appraising him as the potential father of your children (gulp!).

To complicate matters even further, women in this Age Group are intimidating to most men; they prefer women who will make them feel like they are in control. It's your challenge to help a powerful man meet you in the middle, or to empower a weaker man without letting him know that you did it.

> ***Reality Check:*** *"The Catch" is likely to approach his relationships as a man who "knows what he wants and knows how to get it." He will want to be the head of his family, the master of his castle, and the king to his queen. If you come across as too domineering, he might not want to get involved with you. Don't try to control him, and don't criticize his every move.*

Never pursue men in this age bracket; let them pursue you. They already know what they want and they have the power to get it. They prefer to make the important decisions. If they tell you "Yes," you should probably interpret it as a temporary "Okay." Giving them a sense of control is easy, and it will do wonders for your relationship. Let them pick the restaurant, even if you know a better one. Don't correct their grammar. Don't bore them with long stories about your pets (unless you are dating an animal lover!) or come off as a know-it-all. Use your charm and intelligence while staying sharp.

You should also think carefully about having sex too soon with "*The Catch*." If you want this relationship to last, don't treat it like a fling. This brings us to a tricky subject: **Cohabitation**.

Before you agree to live together, you need one of two things:

1. **A ring and a date**
    Or
2. **Two names on the lease**

Cohabitation has been linked to higher divorce rates. Divorce-prone couples tend to first cohabitate, and a number of them do not go on to get married. If they *had* gotten married, the divorce rate would be even higher.

There is a great deal of truth in the adage that men will not buy the cow if they're already getting free milk. Don't let yourself be taken advantage of. If you live with a man for years, you could lose valuable time (remember that clock!) in a situation that is going nowhere.

Before you cohabitate, make sure your partner is committed to a future with you. In other words, you should have an engagement ring and a wedding date, or both of your names should be on the lease. But what happens if he changes his mind or takes too long to marry you? You need to have a deadline. If you've set a wedding date, make him stick to it. If you've simply moved in together, let him know how long you're willing to wait. If that time passes without an ironclad excuse, move on.

With "T*he Catch*," you'll have to be ready for the walk-it-the-way-you-talk-it moment. Many times, you'll do the walking. This tactic might help you claim some of the power from "*The Catch*" and can ignite a more mature, more equal relationship. Or you might have to keep walking.

Most importantly, you should never move in with—much less marry—a man unless you have ART (Acceptance, Respect, and Trust) at all times for each other. We'll talk more about ART in Chapter Five, because the ART model is so important that it truly needs a chapter of its own. These three things will guarantee that the relationship will survive under any and all circumstances.

"In Denial"—Should You Get Involved with a Man Aged 36 or Older?

Older men are a great option for fulfilling your desire for a partner. They're not as dazzled by things like make up and dancing skills. A man in this Age Group will likely have his life established as it will remain, which takes the guesswork out of imagining your future with him. He will probably be emotionally mature and will most likely perceive you as an equal because women mature faster than men. If an older man who has his health and finances in order approaches you, take a good look at what he has to offer.

Of course, age does not always bring wisdom! If your conversations with an older man revolve around his accomplishments and his money, he just might be a juvenile in a man's body, which is the last thing you need.

If you choose to become his ego detective, go into it with your eyes wide open. Everyone is unique, with stories and attitudes that often need encouragement to shine. Take your time getting to know him; you both know the sex will come if all goes well. Make sure you clear up important issues, such as children and childrearing, your long-term future, and your life goals, before things get to serious. Again, you don't want to waste your time on a relationship that is ultimately doomed.

You should note that if a man is more than fifteen years your senior, there may be serious cultural differences between the two of you. He might like different music, have older friends, and live his life at a different pace. There is no reason why you can't enjoy one another's preferences, but you should take them into consideration when you are deciding if he is your Mr. *JUST* Right.

Women Aged 36 and Older: "*Whatever!*"

A mature woman of this age is generally tired of dating and fed up with the games men play. She's at the "*Whatever*, anything will do!" stage. She is largely past her childbearing years, may or may not have children, and has either avoided marriage or gone through a divorce. Women in this Age Group have had to provide for themselves and are facing unfortunate statistics that put their chances of finding a good man up there with their chances of getting into a car accident.

With all this in mind, a woman over the age of 36 is often ready to accept almost anyone out of a sense of desperation to finally settle down. She seeks companionship, predictability, and a stable future.

At the same time, however, her tolerance for nonsense is low. Her past experiences have prepared her for battle and she will not hesitate to tell a man to hit the road. She realizes that she can be unhappy all by herself—she doesn't need a man to make her life even unhappier. She has become set in her ways, which makes it difficult for her to hand over control in a relationship.

And so she is torn between wanting to settle down (with anyone!) and wanting to find a mate who will fully satisfy her. She's open to trying out most relationships, but part of her is still waiting for that White Knight to show up.

The best bet for a woman over the age of 36 is to retain her openness to trying new relationships, but to focus on finding a man who meets her truly important needs. He should bring completion to the areas of her life that she feels are lacking. Most importantly, the two of them should accept, respect, and trust one another for who they really are.

Women in the "*Whatever!*" stage of life should resist the temptation of trying to build a relationship with a man based on what she can do for him. She may have the money, power, fame, opportunities, and experience that most men are eager to exploit. But there's a good chance that he will leave her once he gets what he wants, because their union was never based on acceptance, respect, and trust (ART). This can leave her cynical, making the process of finding her Mr. *JUST* Right even more difficult.

"Whatever!"—Should You Get Involved with a Man Aged 18–25?

Women in this Age Group who date very young men are either desperate or looking for a man that they can control. Often, this relationship consists of clandestine rendezvous. Needless to say, this couple won't last, but they can still offer each other something valuable.

MR. OR MS. JUST RIGHT

Most eighteen- to twenty-five-year-old men who date women who are thirty-six and older are eager to explore their sexuality, are looking for a mother figure to take care of them, and desire a non-permanent situation. These men want someone who can please them, approve of them, spoil them, and give them lots of attention.

The women in these relationships get the companionship and affection they seek, along with a strong, energetic partner in the bedroom. Perhaps they are coming out of a divorce and are looking for a little fun before returning to serious dating.

As he gets older, a younger man will most likely leave an older woman for another woman that he chooses. He has outgrown his need for a mother figure, and no longer wants to be controlled. Instead, he seeks the power and control—or at least the illusion of it—in his household.

If both parties understand that the relationship is a harmless diversion that will eventually fall apart, no one will get too hurt when things end. But women who are 36 and older should remember that finding a lasting partnership with a much younger man is about as likely as being struck by lightening.

"Whatever!"—Should You Get Involved with a Man Aged 26–35?

This is a tough, but potentially fruitful, match. A man in this Age Group is "*The Catch*" and is able to choose women who younger, more compliant, and ready to start a family. You have

OPRAH WINFREY

to use your wiles to make this happen. He can date eighteen-year-olds who will still be relatively young, at least in his eyes, in twenty years. In twenty years, you'll be fifty-six or older! Many available women who likely share similar goals and interests will surround him—and they all want him.

However, "*The Catch*" may be tired of young women who don't know who they are or what they want, or who are inexperienced sexually. He may also be avoiding the nagging "tick-tock" sound that he hears whenever he dates women his own age. These factors can give you an advantage.

You should, by now, know how to seduce a man. We all have those special tricks we use to grab a man's attention and pique his interest, and you've had plenty of time to practice them. Use the confidence you've developed as you've matured to show him that an older woman can be very desirable.

> ***Reality Check:*** *Don't forget that he has to choose you! Men like to think that they are in control of finding their mates, and that they have done well in making that selection. In this type of pairing, the power lies with "The Catch," and you should allow him to exercise his power. Don't try to wrestle him for control, and don't let him realize that you're pursuing him.*

Men in this Age Group may already have children from a previous relationship, which can raise other challenges. His kids or their mother might view you with hostility. If you have children, as well, you will be attempting to blend your families together. At the very least, you will need to be ready to care for his children and make them a large part of your life. Unless you are willing to accept, respect and trust the dynamic of this relationship, you might want to think twice.

"Whatever!"—Should You Get Involved with a Man Aged 36 or Older?

A woman who is 36 or older is most likely quite independent, and would do well to give men in her Age Group careful consideration. The two of you can offer each other affection, companionship, pooled assets, and valuable assistance with conducting the business of life.

The intelligent woman of this age puts her energy into this type of match. Men your age or older provide more security, emotional stability, and financial rewards than younger men can. Most women in the "*Whatever!*" Age Group is not looking for liabilities, and isn't interested in saving a man from himself. Nor do they need someone to save them. Their nurturing days are likely behind them, if that drive ever existed. What they need is a strong partner.

Of course, if your mate has children from a previous marriage, you will have to navigate the complexities of becoming a new part of their lives. If you have children, you will face the added challenge of merging your two families. The good news is that your children are likely to be older by the time you reach this Age Group, and more open to change. As his children come of age, your interactions will his ex-wife will grow less and less frequent. And not all ex-wives are that bad!

What if your partner has never married before? The old adage, "Never marry a bachelor over the age of 40!" has its merits, but remember to take "accepted knowledge" like this with a grain of salt. No two bachelors are the same, and if you are willing to be flexible, you can avoid the second-family complications of previously married men and the wandering eyes of a younger man.

Another potential challenge with this age pairing arises when both parties have developed habits that are hard to break. By this point in your life, you are likely used to doing things a certain way, as is he. Can the two of you accept the things you can't change? Are you willing to change the things you can? Bringing two independent people together raises the need for compromise. But if you are willing to put the work into this relationship, finding a mate within your Age Group is your best choice.

CHAPTER FOUR

FOR MEN ONLY!

First, let's be clear: men and women are different. For example, you probably skipped the "For Women Only!" chapter. But all of the women who pick up this book will read the "For Men Only!" chapter with zero guilt and zero second thoughts.

Don't expect to understand women, and don't expect consistency from them. They dream in color, they speak in code, and they hint at what they want instead of coming out and telling you. They buy certain clothes with the sole purpose of enticing you to take them off. They paint their faces for the battle and they have a higher tolerance for pain. They know things that men don't know, and they band together.

Pursuing a woman often feels like a task that requires the patience of a saint, the wisdom of a sage, and a skin as thick as tree bark. Once you catch her, you might realize that you're not entirely sure who she is. Men wake up looking just as good as they did when they went to bed, while women somehow change during the night. Similarly, a man might begin dating a woman believing she is a certain person, only to find that she is quite different than he thought.

At the same time, there are many types of men, and a man can change both physically and emotionally as the years pass. So if you find women incomprehensible, remember that they often feel the same way about you.

Nobody said this would be easy! Twenty percent of single men want eighty percent of the single women. It's impossible to put yourself in a woman's shoes, especially when the shoes aren't what you're aiming for. So how do you find the perfect mate? You must start by identifying your Age Group:

AGE GROUPS CHART

MEN:

AGE	IDENTITY	POSITION IN THE POWER PLAY
18–25	"Experimenting"	He will accept almost anyone who chooses him.
26–35	"The Catch"	He gets who he chooses, and is at peak mental strength.
36–older	"Oh Snap!"	He depends on his assets and his power to get the person he wants.

If you would like to take a sneak peek at the expectations of women in the corresponding Age Groups, feel free to look through Chapter Three. It can be our little secret. But we will discuss your interactions with them in great detail in this chapter. Before we begin, let me offer you a few words of advice.

The best trick in a man's arsenal is confidence. A man who is clear and consistent about what he wants has an easier time earning a woman's respect. You don't want someone to smother you—you want to be strong and potent. So act like it!

Don't expect women to fall at your feet or to be as fascinated by sex as you are. Of course, it would wonderful for you if human women went into heat occasionally and became desperate for sexual satisfaction from anyone and everyone. No jealousy, no attachments, no paternity suits, right? Sorry, men, that isn't the way it is.

Your needs will change many times throughout your life. Sometimes you'll be the driver and sometimes you'll be the hitchhiker. Sometimes you'll travel toward a new horizon; sometimes you'll get run over. Try to enjoy it all and to learn as much as you can. Be observant and honest with yourself, and continue to stay positive.

What you bring to the party dictates what kind of party it is. The question you have to ask yourself is: "What are you bringing to the table?" If the answer is "the usual," then you can't expect to find an unusual mate. If you want someone special, you have to offer something special. Women are drawn to powerful, confident men who take good care of themselves (hint: make sure you look clean and neat!).

What you give is what you get. If you don't put any effort in your appearance, how can you expect to attract someone who does? If you don't behave responsibly, you'll have a hard time finding a responsible mate. Appraise yourself correctly and often. If it's broke, fix it.

We all have a specific type of person we find attractive. Mostly, it's the familiar. Perhaps you like women who remind you of your first crush. Men in particular are visual animals, and sexual attraction plays a huge role in their relationships. This is natural and normal, but don't let it override your judgment. It's perfectly fine to stick with your "type"—just make sure she offers more than a pretty face.

You must remember that physical beauty fades, and even sexual chemistry can cool. After a few years, sleeping with Miss America might feel like sleeping with your cousin. The hundredth time will be nothing like the first. Remember the words of Billy Bob Thornton, who had a sexual relationship with the stunning Angelina Jolie for years: "Sex doesn't have to be with a model to be good. As a matter of fact, sometimes with the model, the actress, the 'sexiest person in the world,' it may be literally like "doing a couch." Not tactful, but true.

And don't fool yourself into thinking you'll always be as attractive as you are today. Your eyes will give out, your hair will fall out, and your belly will stick out. It's estimated that

MR. OR MS. JUST RIGHT

with every decade, a man's erect penis position will descend by a 10% angle. Think about that the next time you find yourself critiquing a woman's appearance.

Be realistic about the kinds of women you pursue. Don't waste your time shooting over your head or trying to seduce someone else's girlfriend. If you date a married woman—or, far worse, an underage girl—you might just end up with a shotgun blast to the groin. I doubt you'll think it's worth it.

Don't be the villain in a couple's break-up. If you convince a woman to cheat *with* you, what makes you think she won't cheat *on* you? When you know the woman you want is in a dead-end relationship, try to be patient. The good ones don't stay out of the game for long, so after you give her an appropriate cooling-off period, make your move.

You've got to stay positive. Don't say, "Women: can't live with 'em...pass the beer nuts." Don't belittle your mate. Instead, be thankful for the fact that you have a partner in building a relationship and raising children—two of the most difficult endeavors you will ever undertake. When in doubt, keep your mouth shut.

It will all be worth it in the end. Half the men over the age of 80 who are in a relationship still have sex more than twice a month. Not a bad prospect, right? It's certainly better than growing old alone and celibate.

Men Aged 18–25: "*Experimenting*"

Men of this age are discovering themselves, their bodies, and the world around them; they are open and eager to try new things. In this Age Group, men just want to have fun exploring the unknown—and sometimes the dangerous. To them, a long-term relationship begins when someone says "long-term relationship." Before that, it's just a casual fling. "Until Christmas" is probably a frightening commitment for "*Experimenting*." It means finding a present, introducing her to the family, raising expectations....

This age bracket attracts women of all ages for a number of reasons ranging from pure physical desire to youthful romance.

Women of a similar age ("*Innocence*") are available through school or work. They tend to project their *innocence* onto a man, imagining him as the gentle poet. Or they may fantasize that he is a little dangerous and knows some wild things. If you're just looking for a quick liaison, it's best to allow them to believe whatever they want.

Slightly older women (aged 26–35) find young men to be more pliable—they imagine molding him into more of what they want in a mate. A woman of this age can exert more control over a younger man than an older man, and can even just use him for sex until the "right one" appears. Everybody wins!

Much older women are usually in it for the young flesh. Relationships with them are unlikely to last long or move beyond the physical. Since young men rarely turn down available sexual experiences, you might as well enjoy it while it lasts.

So have fun, but remember this: Whatever type of relationship you enter, **it's best to move on before making a lasting commitment**.

Enjoy being in love, should that phenomenon come your way. Love is the most blissful, ecstatic part of existence—the joyous connection of two people who know that their happiness depends on being together. But it's highly doubtful that you're ready to commit to her.

> ***Reality Check:*** *Don't confuse "falling in love" with long-term love. First love tends to focus on sex and excitement; long-term love is a process, a roller coaster, a journey into the unknown, and a focus on the moon. As the Tao tells us, "In Action, Watch the Timing."*

Idealism is great when matched with realism, but an idealistic couple with their heads in the clouds will probably panic and self-destruct like a deer in the headlights when the inevitable troubles of life hit them.

The Great Escape!

You can get out of almost any situation by citing your age. "I didn't know!" "I had absolutely no idea you felt that way!" "I'm sorry, I just didn't realize the consequences of what I was doing!" These are phrases that will serve you well as you plan your escape from a tricky situation.

If it's the "morning after" you and a girl you were formerly "just friends" with had drunken monkey sex, take it in stride. Don't let the fact that you're feeling weird and guilty be a reason for you not to nail each other again before the discussion occurs about what a big mistake it was. Always remember your escape phrases (hint, try using "Damn, I was *still* really drunk!")

However...

There are a few consequences that you cannot smooth over with a glib line or two. So please make this your watchword: **LATEX**.

Yes, it feels better without it. Yes, you think you're invincible. Yes, she's told you that she can't get pregnant at this point in her cycle. Yes, she claims she's on the pill.

No.

A woman can conceive at any time, regardless of where she is in her cycle. Sometimes we ovulate twice in a single month. And sometimes she's lying about being on birth control. Be smart about protection unless you want to be a father long before you're ready for it.

And the consequences might even extend far beyond having a baby. You can catch a wide range of diseases—some which might even kill you. So remember your watchword, and use a condom. No amount of fun is worth destroying your life.

Finally, please say "no" to drugs. You don't need to start up a dead-end street, especially when you have so many options ahead of you.

"Experimenting"—Should You Get Involved with a Woman Aged 18–25?

If a man of this age is dating a woman of the same age group, she has most likely chosen him. Women aged 18–25 hold the power in these relationships. She might want him for sex, companionship, protection, a friend, a possible mate, or a back-up plan. Whatever the reason, enjoy reaping the benefits of her choice!

Whatever power you have in this relationship comes from your curiosity, persistence, sincerity, strength, similar goals and interests, and desire. While such qualities are attractive, they come nowhere near the potency of "vagina power," especially for "*Innocence.*"

Women your age are wanted by 80% of the horny men looking for easy sex. So that'd be 80% of all men. She knows she's attractive (at minimum, to some men), she knows she's fertile; she knows her power lies in her unlocking and surrendering her physical restraints. She chooses who she wants, for whatever reason she wants.

So how do you catch the eye of "*Innocence*"? Put yourself out there! Groom yourself well, invest in a nice set of wheels, and hang out in locations where you're likely to find her. If you want to pick a juicy apple, spend your time in apple orchards.

Keep in mind that the woman in this age pairing will normally be choosing you. If you seem too eager, you might blow your chances with her. Don't leave messages on her answering machine. Don't follow her around. And don't be discouraged by the competition; there's a good chance she doesn't know what the hell she wants, or will eventually accept you as a casual hookup. But always remember: **"No"** ***never* means, "yes."**

There is minimal discretion expected from a young man who is curious about what he wants and motivated by the desire for sexual experiences. Some men proposition every girl they meet: "Hi, would you have sex with me?" Naturally, the vast majority of women tell them to get lost, but some might agree. He may have caught her at the right moment, or perhaps she has a "please the world" complex. Maybe she told her friends she'd say "yes" at the very next opportunity. These men might be getting pity sex, angry sex, aloof sex, or mercy sex … but it's still sex. The more women they ask, the better their chances.

Find out what works for you. Try honesty. Be creative. There are so many enjoyable facets of the courting ritual: the flirting, the hunt, the moment you know the deal is sealed, the laughter at your lousy jokes, and the intense stares into her beautiful eyes…. Then there's the testosterone boost you get when a woman wants you; there's no doubt that it revs you up and gives you confidence. Everyone enjoys feeling desirable and accepted. And, of course, you'll have an orgasm that you didn't have to give yourself, which is better than beer, music, or the playoffs.

Don't beat yourself up because you don't want to beat yourself off. You're a dog and when you're thrown some meat, you eat. Good boy! You may realize that "*Innocence*" is just using you, but you'll still go along with it. That doesn't make you a bad guy—it simply makes you a guy.

If you want more than a one-night stand, your best bet is to explore a relationship with a friend who is as intelligent and healthy as you, and who has a successful life, independent of you. Find a person who admires and honors you. A perpetual motion machine would be good, too!

Warning: Prepare for emotions, some of which you've never felt before. Men and women in this Age Group are both exploring themselves. Don't follow roads that you know will lead to heartbreak, obsession, or gloomy poetry. The horizontal mambo can quickly become the tangled tango. If she moves on, live with it.

There is a tendency to fall in love with one's lover, especially one's first lover. Time spent exploring the bliss of young romance is a fabulous experience. Then comes the letdown of reality setting in: the hot and cold cycles, the conversations and habits that annoy you, and (usually) the breakup. Don't discount this wonderful ride, but don't take it too seriously.

As we discussed, you probably aren't quite ready for a serious commitment. Men who get married in their twenties are generally looking for an unlimited supply of sex, and relationships built largely on physical desire have no chance of standing the test of time. But make no mistake about it—she's getting ready.

She doesn't have 20 years to stumble along. For men, becoming a father in one's late 30s is close to ideal; for women, becoming a mother in one's late 30s is a medical miracle. If she isn't looking for marriage yet, she will be soon, and she is highly unlikely to pick "*Experimenting*" as the father of her children.

The odds of ending up with your first lover are very long. You know that. She knows that. A marriage between "*Innocence*" and "*Experimenting*" would be set in quicksand.

So saddle up and enjoy the ride!

"Experimenting"—Should You Get Involved with a Woman Aged 26–35?

A woman between the ages of 26 and 35 generally dates a man aged 18 to 25 only if she is lonely, wants sex, or needs to control her partner. She's had one or more relationships go sour and is either looking for power or looking to misbehave. Of course, rebound sex can be the lustiest. Where's the downside in helping her work out her issues?

Bear in mind that a woman in this Age Group will probably get tired of you easily, make your life boring (or chaotic, if she's been hurt or damaged in the past), or force you into endless conversations about commitment and the future of your relationship. She may be critical of you and blame you for not being the man she really wants. She may use sex as a weapon—an emasculating tactic. She may get pregnant, perhaps even on purpose. Beware, "*Experimenting*," you may be in over your head.

Fortunately, women of this age generally understand that the younger man is not inclined to build a mature bond or long-term relationship with an older woman. He's exploring his sexuality with someone who's already done some exploring and might have a thing or two to teach him.

While there is conquest and ego acceptance in this dynamic, neither person in is likely to get what he or she really wants. And the larger the age gap (for instance, an eighteen-year-old man with a thirty-five-year-old woman), the more dysfunctional these couples tend to be. It's highly improbable that you will find your Ms. *JUST* Right in this relationship.

"Experimenting"—Should You Get Involved with a Woman Aged 36 or Older?

Women aged 36 and older who date men who are much younger are, quite simply, desperate. Be it sex or companionship, they need it urgently. They are looking for confirmation that they are still attractive. And perhaps they are! If experience is your only sexual goal, this is the place to go. They'll be comfortable with their bodies, not afraid of getting pregnant, and aware of what is expected of them. The older woman can be a very useful sexual tutor.

She may be eccentric. She may have cats. But on the other hand, you may not even have to pay for dinner.

The downside is that older women are set in their ways and usually desire a huge degree of control, particularly in liaisons with younger men. They come with emotional baggage and bad habits—it's nearly impossible to reach the age of 36 without them. For the younger man, this relationship will not go far. Being the boy toy, he can't practice being the man. And in the end, no man wants to remain a boy. Even (and possibly especially) in the bedroom, she will want to dominate you. Unless you're very subservient by nature, that will get old quickly.

But in the meantime, it's often good sailing on a clear day.

Men Aged 26–35: "*The Catch*"

This age range is a very exciting time for men, because they have come into their full power. "*The Catch*" most likely is out of school, is fit and healthy, and has a career. He's also developed a level of common sense that, combined with his relative youth, puts him at his mental peak.

At this age, men are probably also thinking about settling down—and women know it. Women also realize that while "*The Catch*" thinks he knows exactly what he wants, he's still somewhat pliable and open to change. When men in this Age Group choose a woman, they are ready and willing to satisfy her or at least meet her needs.

These qualities make him a highly desirable partner for women of every Age Group. There's a reason he's called "*The Catch*," after all! This is the ideal age for a man to choose a partner, although some may not be ready until later (if at all).

Men in this Age Group enjoy pursuing women, and a little bit of persistence can bring them great rewards. Be careful about how you present yourself. Although women claim they like men who have a sense of humor and are fun be with, they're really looking for something else. They want someone who is both attractive and deep. Deep enough to understand the woman that she is; attractive enough to get sweaty with.

Whatever juvenile charm got you through the teenage years should get packed away. It's unbecoming in a man of this age.

If you aren't looking for a permanent relationship, be honest with her. Don't tell a woman you love her to get her into bed. You might feel like you love her in the heat of the moment, but nothing you say during intercourse counts! Women of all ages are trying to catch you. Some will trick you, some will grill you like a homicide detective, and some will try to drag you down some rainbow path in their minds. You should know yourself by now, so keep things real, or women might read things into your character that aren't truly there.

OPRAH WINFREY

If You Decide to Get Marry: The Hard Facts

You have to think long and hard about whether marriage and a family are in your best interests at this age. Are you mature enough for mature matters?

Most importantly, you have to take great care in choosing the potential mother of your children. This decision will impact your choice far more than the schools you went to, the awards you won, and the job you got. Try not to let your dick do all the talking.

You don't have to pursue the youngest of the women you're attracted to, or the one with the largest breasts. You don't need to say, "yes" to the older woman who looked a lot better at the bar. You don't have to cheer up the melancholic or be infected by the sickly. You don't have to be trapped or manipulated by the damaged.

Make sure you do everything you can to **up the odds that your marriage will succeed**. In earlier decades, marriages in which men were at least seven to ten years older than the woman had approximately a ninety percent survival rate. In the 1980's, eighty-one percent of college graduates we were over the age of 26 years when they got married were still married 20 years later. But only forty-nine percent of high school graduates who were under the age of 26 when they wed in the 1980s were still married 20 years later.

So find a mate of the appropriate age that went to college, shares your goals, and prays to the Lord to forgive your stupidity.

Cohabitation: The Double-Edged Sword

Living with a woman takes care of your sexual needs and saves money. It's a good deal for the guy. But things can easily go wrong. If the relationship ends, you'll have to decide how to split your assets. Who keeps the apartment or house? Who gets the TV you purchased together? It's helpful to write these things down in advance, but few couples actually do this, and you'll still have to negotiate about many things.

Keeping your own place where you can escape and chill out is always a sensible idea. If a relationship is still developing, it's good to have some space. Remember, it's much easier to move in than to move out. Things get purchased together, pets show up, your rent will double when you leave, and the breakup will leave a bad vibe with both of you.

It may seem like "it's cheaper to keep her," but you should think about all of the logistics that come into play with cohabitation. In the long run, it might not be worth saving a bit of money. Have an exit strategy. Chances are good that she does.

Whatever you do, keep an eye on the clock. Your nine years of being "*The Catch*" will go by quickly. Enjoy them while you can.

"The Catch"—Should You Get Involved with a Woman Aged 18–25?

For men in this Age Group who are looking for someone with whom to build and grow or possibly start a family, women between the ages of 18 and 25 are a great choice. These women will be fertile and developed, aware of their sexuality, and innocent (at least in your eyes). They will also have a natural inclination to let an older man take charge—in other words, they will allow a man to be a man.

You may find yourself solving a younger woman's problems or holding her hand as she sobs over something her girlfriend said or a minor issue like being cut from the cheerleading squad. You have to at least pretend to be concerned. Try to read her cues and listen to her. Use your instincts to find out exactly who and what you're dealing with. If you want a peek at her future, check out her mother; chances are good she'll look like her in 25 years, and possibly even act like her.

The process can be frustrating and time-consuming, but in the meantime, she'll probably provide the "nookie" relatively quickly to an older, more experienced man. Waiting for sex is one thing, but to put up with catering to the needs of a young woman without having sex will destroy the relationship. "*Innocence*" can be a handful, and you're trying to focus on your career, health, and other important aspects of your life at this point. You need sexual release, and she needs the growth that a sexual relationship brings. The younger woman is innocent and also becoming—in that you get to hump her into becoming all that she can be!

> ***Reality Check:*** *A younger woman who thinks she is the only one doing the choosing with "The Catch" is out of touch, spoiled, and running with blinders on. You may find her very enticing, but you are also doing the choosing during this period of your life. You've got the ball, so to speak. Young women with this mentality are like a very expensive bag of candy: not filling, but quite yummy at the moment.*

You'll need to be patient with "*Innocence*," because she's likely to be inexperienced in life and relationships. Too often, she is still looking for a White Knight or Prince Charming. She just got boobs a few years ago. Her finances aren't very stable. When problems arise, she may be unequipped to work through them. It's a wonder that women in this age group represent the largest number of brides.

If her charming personality gives way to fits of anger, tears, and irrationality, you might want to hit the door. Choose a young woman who has a good head on her shoulders. "I wanna have a good time, have fun, be successful, and be nothing like my folks!" is not the philosophy of a suitable mate, no matter how great her body looks. It's like drafting a high-school basketball star into the NBA—it's a wild card.

On the other hand, sometimes you have to take a chance, and the best ones don't stay single long. Younger women have much to offer. They don't have as many relationship scars. They're as juicy as a persimmon and as sweet as a fig, and they will stay healthy longer than older women. They're likely to respect you already because of your age and social standing, and possibly admire and trust you. Being with her can be like shooting ducks in a barrel (only you have to take care of the barrel until you die).

Serious men have serious decisions to make about life and must consider a woman's goals and interests, her DNA, and her position—both in the world and on the sheets—when choosing a spouse. And don't forget your list! Does she fulfill at least 5 of the 10 qualities you want in a mate?

Don't expect perfection. Don't expect omnipotence. Don't expect a woman who will bear your children, be the perfect mother for them, keep you interested sexually, make your life easier, and carry you through your old age. It doesn't happen like that. Be realistic in your desires, or you will never be satisfied. And if your relationship isn't built on Acceptance, Respect, and Trust, no amount of physical desire can save it.

"The Catch"—Should You Get Involved with a Woman Aged 26–35?

You have to use your judgment with a woman in this Age Group, just as you would with an 18–25 year old. The difference is that a woman of your own age will be surer of her goals and interests than "*Innocence*" is. She'll be less likely to fall apart over minor details like arguments with friends. She will have finished her education and will no longer be dependent on her parents. Hopefully, she will have thought about what she really wants in life, particularly when it comes to starting a family. She'll still be healthy and is more likely to be sexually uninhibited than a younger woman.

But she may also be spoiled, hypocritical, stubborn, and arrogant. Many women in this age group think they still possess the power of "*Innocence*," but in reality, their days of "I choose you, I get you" are over. You have the power in this relationship. Use it, but don't abuse it. If you're not ready to be exclusive with her, beware of conversations that start with words like "If we're not going to see other people...." She might be trying to wrestle your choice away from you.

Modern society has seen an interesting change in the concept of age. Throughout most of human history (and in many cultures today), a woman over the age of 30 would be considered far past her prime. Today's westernized woman lives a longer, healthier life, and has access to birth control. She can still easily bear children at that age, and often does not want to start a family until she hits her 30s and has accomplished her goals.

Because of this, she rarely realizes that she is no longer as powerful as she was when she was younger, or that she will be past her prime by the time she hits 36. But at some point, she will begin to understand that finding a partner, a father for her children, and a source of support in her later years has become more difficult, and that she's running out of time. Even if she's hot, stacked, and double-jointed, you will be the one doing the choosing in this age pairing.

> ***Reality Check:*** *Be very cautious with a woman between the ages of 26 and 35 who wants to start a family, because her biological alarm is going off. She's hit the five-more-years-of-sleep button on her evolutionary clock, but she can't wait forever. And watch yourself—accidentally getting her pregnant will be a disaster. You're not a kid anymore, so don't act like one.*

Women are impressed by money, power, possessions, strength, humor, and charm. (The list gets longer as they keep drinking.) If you have these attributes, she will be interested in getting you to commit to her, and might present herself as someone she's not in order to seal the deal. Try to view your partners objectively, and read between the lines. When the mask comes off, trust and respect will be a thing of the past.

If "*The Catch*" is looking for a mate he can relate to easily, share his life journey with, and meet halfway in making important decisions, he is very likely to find his ideal mate in a woman between the ages of 26 and 35. Remember, you can't keep dating young girls forever. You aren't over the hill yet, but you'll soon be a decade (or more) older than a twenty-year-old. When you hit the next Age Group, society will begin to view you as a dirty old letch. It's not an attractive look.

"The Catch"—Should You Get Involved with a Woman Aged 36 or Older?

Men between the ages of 26 and 35 who still need direction or some security in their lives will often end up with women who are 36 or older. Men of this type do not want to assert their full power as a man; they know that the power to choose who they want to be with lies in their hands, but they are voluntarily surrendering it.

As this type of relationship progresses, the man may make himself believe that he is in control of it, even though he knows in his heart that this isn't true. But these men are searching for security above all else—it is more important to them than exerting their full power.

If that is the case, this age dynamic often works better than one might think. It fulfills the man's deepest needs while giving the woman a virile husband who is past the foolishness of extreme youth. Religious or family goals met together can give this relationship an unshakeable bond.

Just remember, men, that you might be turning 46 when she turns 60. "Wanna play some shuffleboard, honey?"

Men Aged 36 and Older: *"Oh Snap!"*

Men over the age of 35 are in the "*Oh Snap!*" state of mind—as in "*Oh Snap*: No Money, No Honey!" Many will entice women with their assets (their cars, houses, careers, fame, money, and opportunities). If they have plenty of these resources, they might be inclined to collect women, using lies if necessary to get them into bed.

Age does not necessarily bring wisdom. There are many adolescents in forty-year-old bodies. Are you truly prepared for a mature partnership with a woman? If this is your first attempt at a permanent relationship, you should understand that you bring a lot of baggage with you: habits and manners that will not mesh perfectly with women of any age. The old saw "Never marry a bachelor over the age of 40!" recognizes that certain men remain single for decades because they simply aren't willing to accommodate the needs of a partner.

Of course, there are many men in this age bracket who realize that they have waited too long to settle down and are sincere about sorting their lives out. If this describes you, then you are a good match for women of any age. Just remember that most women who date men in your Age Group are not interested in you because of your looks, your sex drive, or your personality. They want your lifestyle and to use your assets to create a family or enjoy the pleasures of life.

If a man who finds himself in the "*Oh Snap!*" category wants to settle down, he will most likely end up with a woman in the second age bracket (26–35). This pairing works for a number of reasons. He will be able to relate to her emotional strength, goals, and intelligence, since women mature more quickly than men. She will be very interested in starting a family (that clock keeps ticking!), which can fulfill both parties' dreams.

The other Age Groups don't offer the ideal match. The majority of older men would be quite happy to date a woman under the age of 26, be it for fun, for control, for sex, or for her fertility. But unless you are wealthy or famous, you're unlikely to get such a young woman. If you select a woman in your own Age Group, the odds of starting a family with her are low. Your partnership will be more of a merging of assets and bills, as well as an assurance of companionship as you grow older.

"Oh Snap!"—Should You Get Involved with a Woman Aged 18–25?

Who wouldn't, right? But let's keep things real. If you want a woman of this Age Group, your assets are the only things that will get her for you. Don't think she's dating you because of your cute button nose. There are plenty of adorable noses attached to strong young bodies.

A woman who is ten years (or more) younger than her partner is interested in him for security, comfort, and stability; she's not in it for the sex or the excitement, although those may be part of the package. Don't kid yourself. If you have limited assets, forget about pursuing women in this Age Group. You'll just make a fool of yourself.

Even if you are very wealthy, you might want to think long and hard about choosing a woman from the "*Innocence*" category. If you're thinking long-term, you're looking at long odds.

Women of this age are unpredictable, and they are in high demand. They are being approached by both sixteen-year-olds who don't think they're too young and fifty-year-olds who don't think they're too old. They have countless options, but they rarely know what they want because they have limited experience. They'll have questionable taste in music, friends, and entertainment. If you have accumulated enough wealth to tempt "*Innocence*," there's a good chance you have gained some common sense along the way. Try to employ it here.

"Oh Snap!"—Should You Get Involved with a Woman Aged 26–35?

This is the most difficult of all the age pairings. Power is the force that drives the mating game. And here, no one has the power.

If one of these parties demands the power, the relationship is ultimately doomed. The man can give up his control, which is a formula for emasculation. The woman can give up her power, which is a formula for abuse. In the end, one of the parties will resent the other. If they don't have children, this couple is not likely to remain together.

With children, this age pairing can divide their power fairly if Acceptance, Respect, and Trust are present. Women in this group are ready to raise a family, and can be quite calculating in pursuing that goal. Their desire to have children may make them more amenable to accepting your control. But bear in mind that they're likely to have strong opinions about childrearing and will often demand pre-nuptial agreements.

> ***Reality Check:*** *If a woman is more than ten years your junior, your position is comparable to courting a woman under the age of 26. Your assets will be the major factor for a woman of that age. You are no longer "The Catch," and she still has several options open to her.*

"Oh Snap!"—Should You Get Involved with a Woman Aged 36 or Older?

If your ages are similar and you aren't interested in having children at this point, this can be a great match. The stress of raising young kids is behind you. Both of you have established your means of support. You can enjoy each other's company and share life's burdens.

There is an old saying: "A woman marries a man expecting he will change, but he doesn't. A man marries a woman expecting that she won't change, and she does." This is less of a pitfall with people over the age of 35. Her character is fully formed, so you'll know exactly what you're getting into.

If she's high-maintenance now, she'll be high-maintenance years from now. If she loves to bake, you'll be eating a lot of cookies in your old age.

This is usually the best group for an older man to court, and it works well for both parties. Often, the woman has children who need a man around. She knows she will probably outlive you, and is looking for security in her old age, as well as comfort and companionship. In return, she will ease your loneliness, offer you sexual gratification, and often bring her own assets into the relationship.

On the other hand, women who are 36 or older generally have baggage: personality quirks that might not match your needs, children whom you must persuade to accept you, sexual tendencies that may not suit you, and pets that get on your nerves and sleep in your bed. They also tend to be inflexible in various areas, such as politics, health, finances, and lifestyle.

The good news is that many women of this Age Group are available, and longer courtships are the norm among older couples, so you'll be able to take your time searching for the *JUST* Right partner. Don't thoughtlessly give away your heart, half of your assets, and your time to a woman who isn't worth it. Having no deal is better than having a bad deal.

You may be entering the relationship with your own baggage. Men in this Age Group have often been married before and are hoping to avoid making the same errors with their second wives. In 2008, 46% of all marriages involved at least one spouse who is remarrying. Hope springs eternal!

So learn from your past mistakes. Communication is paramount here; a woman of your age has some standards that you will have to meet. There are things she can't live with or without. Which one will you be? Flow. Grow. Find the partner you need, and be the partner she needs.

CHAPTER FIVE

ART, THE FOUNDATION OF TRUE LOVE

NOTE: IF YOU are in search of a temporary relationship, you can skip this section of the book, because it is not relevant to your position. Most people who are interested in a temporary relationship are with someone for little more than convenience. Usually, the parties involved will rely on physical or material things like money, power, fame, and sex to pursue the other person.

The elements of **ART**—**A**cceptance, **R**espect, and **T**rust—are the building blocks of **A**ctual **R**eal **T**rue love. They apply not only to romantic relationships, but also to the bonds that exist between family, friends, neighbors, co-workers, colleagues ... the list goes on. Any kind of strong connection must be based on ART.

The Elements

We all know the dictionary definitions of acceptance, respect, and trust, but what do those words mean in the context of a relationship? How do they come together to bring ART to your marriage? We'll examine each element below.

Acceptance

It's impossible to truly love someone if you don't fully accept who he or she is. People are complex creatures, made up of many different beliefs and choices. Refusing to accept certain aspects of your partner's character is the same thing as rejecting him or her completely, because those aspects that you can't tolerate are part of who your mate is.

Until you fully embrace each other—flaws and all—you cannot hope to find Actual Real True love together. You must always be there for each other, no matter what the circumstances, and especially in your times of need.

Respect

Partners who don't respect one another and treat each other with respect will not stay together for long. No one truly loves someone that they can't respect. If you feel an ounce of contempt for someone, it will poison your heart toward him or her.

Similarly, no one likes to be disparaged or looked down upon. You may think you're being subtle when you disrespect your partner, but people tend to pick up on very tiny cues, particularly in a romantic relationship. If you belittle your mate, don't be surprised when he or she decides to find someone who won't.

Trust

Imagine trying to build an enduring marriage with someone you don't trust. How can you raise children, manage your finances, plan for the future, and enjoy the company of a person you can't rely upon? How can you kiss your spouse goodbye when you leave on a business trip if you fear he or she might cheat on you while you're away?

Without full trust, a couple will never come together as a cohesive team. They won't be able to meet each other in the middle on important decisions, because they won't have faith in one another. Your spouse should be your other half—your helper and your support system—not the person you always have to watch.

Is Your Relationship Built Upon ART?

These ART elements must be earned through hard work. They cannot be rented, leased, purchased, or sold. Establishing ART is a delicate process, and it must be handled with care and caution. If any of the three elements are missing, the parties involved need to focus on reestablishing the one they have lost. The lack of one ART element could disrupt or even destroy the others, which could bring a promising relationship to a heartbreaking end.

Most of us envision ending up in a permanent relationship. We want to spend our lives with the right partner, working together to pursue common goals. In the previous chapters, we discovered which age pairings work best together. But that's just the beginning—your next step is to make sure ART exists in your relationship. Only then can you be sure that you have found your Mr. or Ms. *JUST* Right.

So how exactly do you determine if you have the elements of ART in your relationship? This book has done the hard work for you! The quizzes below will help you take a deeper look at different facets of your relationship, and will show you whether or not ART exists between you and your mate. To help you keep everything straight, you should call yourself "Partner 1" and "Partner 2." Pick a number and stick with it!

Answer the questions honestly, because lying serves no purpose here. You're trying to diagnose your relationship, not just pass a test for the sake of passing it. So take a deep breath and dive in.

TEST 1: ACCEPTANCE
PARTNER 1

PARTNER 1, this test is for you! The questions are about how YOU treat or view your mate, PARTNER 2. Circle the answer that best describes your situation.

1) PARTNER 2's physical attractiveness is the least important factor for me in our relationship.

Answer:	Always	Usually	Sometimes	Rarely	Never
Score:	5	4	3	2	1

2) I have no concerns about PARTNER 2's lifestyle.

Answer:	Always	Usually	Sometimes	Rarely	Never
Score:	5	4	3	2	1

3) I accept PARTNER 2's children and pets.

Answer:	Always	Usually	Sometimes	Rarely	Never
Score:	5	4	3	2	1

4) I introduce PARTNER 2 to people who are important to me, like my friends and family.

Answer:	Always	Usually	Sometimes	Rarely	Never
Score:	5	4	3	2	1

5) I appreciate and acknowledge PARTNER 2's career choice.

Answer:	Always	Usually	Sometimes	Rarely	Never
Score:	5	4	3	2	1

PARTNER 1's Acceptance Test, Total Score:

	+		+		+		+		=	
Question 1		Question 2		Question 3		Question 4		Question 5		**Total**

TEST 1: ACCEPTANCE
PARTNER 2

PARTNER 2, this test is for you! The questions are about how YOU treat or view your mate, PARTNER 1. Circle the answer that best describes your situation.

1) How often do you hug and kiss PARTNER 1?

Answer:	Always	Usually	Sometimes	Rarely	Never
Score:	5	4	3	2	1

2) How often do you invite PARTNER 1 to your friends' or relatives' homes?

Answer:	Always	Usually	Sometimes	Rarely	Never
Score:	5	4	3	2	1

3) If PARTNER 1 has pets and children, do you spend time with them?

Answer:	Always	Usually	Sometimes	Rarely	Never
Score:	5	4	3	2	1

4) Do you accept PARTNER 1's habits (such as smoking, eating, drinking, or cursing)?

Answer:	Always	Usually	Sometimes	Rarely	Never
Score:	5	4	3	2	1

5) Do you love spending time with PARTNER 1?

Answer:	Always	Usually	Sometimes	Rarely	Never
Score:	5	4	3	2	1

PARTNER 2's Acceptance Test, Total Score:

	+		+		+		+		=	
Question 1		Question 2		Question 3		Question 4		Question 5		**Total**

TEST 2: RESPECT
PARTNER 1

PARTNER 1, this test is for you! The questions are about how YOU treat or view your mate, PARTNER 2. Circle the answer that best describes your situation.

1) When PARTNER 2's phone rings, I _____ ask for permission before I answer it.

Answer:	Always	Usually	Sometimes	Rarely	Never
Score:	5	4	3	2	1

2) When PARTNER 2 is communicating with me, I _____ look into his/her eyes.

Answer:	Always	Usually	Sometimes	Rarely	Never
Score:	5	4	3	2	1

3) I feel that PARTNER 2 _____ shares household chores fairly and responsibly.

Answer:	Always	Usually	Sometimes	Rarely	Never
Score:	5	4	3	2	1

4) I _____ take PARTNER 2's feelings into consideration before reacting to him/her or expressing myself.

Answer:	Always	Usually	Sometimes	Rarely	Never
Score:	5	4	3	2	1

5) I _____ communicate with PARTNER 2 before making important decisions.

Answer:	Always	Usually	Sometimes	Rarely	Never
Score:	5	4	3	2	1

PARTNER 1's Respect Test, Total Score:

	+		+		+		+		=	
Question 1		Question 2		Question 3		Question 4		Question 5		**Total**

TEST 2: RESPECT
PARTNER 2

PARTNER 2, this test is for you! The questions are about how YOU treat or view your mate, PARTNER 1. Circle the answer that best describes your situation.

1) I _____ ask permission before answering PARTNER 1's phone.

Answer:	Always	Usually	Sometimes	Rarely	Never
Score:	5	4	3	2	1

2) I _____ look into PARTNER 1's eyes when he/she is speaking to me.

Answer:	Always	Usually	Sometimes	Rarely	Never
Score:	5	4	3	2	1

3) PARTNER 1 _____ shares our household chores fairly and responsibly.

Answer:	Always	Usually	Sometimes	Rarely	Never
Score:	5	4	3	2	1

4) I _____ consider PARTNER 1's feelings before expressing myself or reacting to him/her.

Answer:	Always	Usually	Sometimes	Rarely	Never
Score:	5	4	3	2	1

5) Before making important decisions, I _____ consult PARTNER 1.

Answer:	Always	Usually	Sometimes	Rarely	Never
Score:	5	4	3	2	1

PARTNER 2's Respect Test, Total Score:

	+		+		+		+		=	
Question 1		Question 2		Question 3		Question 4		Question 5		**Total**

TEST 3: TRUST
PARTNER 1

PARTNER 1, this test is for you! The questions are about how YOU treat or view your mate, PARTNER 2. Circle the answer that best describes your situation.

1) I can _____ rely upon what PARTNER 2 is telling me.

Answer:	Always	Usually	Sometimes	Rarely	Never
Score:	5	4	3	2	1

2) I can _____ leave PARTNER 2 alone with my friends.

Answer:	Always	Usually	Sometimes	Rarely	Never
Score:	5	4	3	2	1

3) I _____ have access to PARTNER 2's accounts and financial information

Answer:	Always	Usually	Sometimes	Rarely	Never
Score:	5	4	3	2	1

4) I _____ have key(s) to PARTNER 2's home or car.

Answer:	Always	Usually	Sometimes	Rarely	Never
Score:	5	4	3	2	1

OPRAH WINFREY

5) PARTNER 2 _____ allows me to leave my things at his/her home.

Answer:	Always	Usually	Sometimes	Rarely	Never
Score:	5	4	3	2	1

PARTNER 1's Trust Test, Total Score:

	+		+		+		+		=	
Question 1		Question 2		Question 3		Question 4		Question 5		**Total**

TEST 3: TRUST PARTNER 2

PARTNER 2, this test is for you! The questions are about how YOU treat or view your mate, PARTNER 1. Circle the answer that best describes your situation.

1) PARTNER 1 _____ gives me trustworthy information.

Answer:	Always	Usually	Sometimes	Rarely	Never
Score:	5	4	3	2	1

2) I _____ feel comfortable leaving PARTNER 1 alone with my friends.

Answer:	Always	Usually	Sometimes	Rarely	Never
Score:	5	4	3	2	1

3) PARTNER 1's accounts and financial information are _____ accessible to me.

Answer:	Always	Usually	Sometimes	Rarely	Never
Score:	5	4	3	2	1

4) PARTNER 1 _____ lets me have the key(s) to his/her home or car.

Answer:	Always	Usually	Sometimes	Rarely	Never
Score:	5	4	3	2	1

5) I _____ leave my things at PARTNER 1's home.

Answer:	Always	Usually	Sometimes	Rarely	Never
Score:	5	4	3	2	1

(Likert scale, Christian Vanek 2012).

PARTNER 2's Trust Test, Total Score:

	+		+		+		+		=	
Question 1		Question 2		Question 3		Question 4		Question 5		**Total**

ADDING THE SCORES

Write the total score for each partner from each test (Acceptance, Respect, and Trust) in the corresponding **ART Score** brackets below to determine your final grade.

ART Score Brackets

Partner 1

Acceptance: _____

Respect: _____

Trust: _____

Partner 2

Acceptance: _____

Respect: _____

Trust: _____

Now that both of the ART Scores are in the ART Score brackets, add up each partner's ART Scores to get your individual **Grand Total ART Score**s. Write down both of your Grand Total ART Scores below:

Grand Total ART Scores

Partner 1: _____   **Partner 2:** _____

Add these two Grand Total ART Scores together for your **Final Score**: _____

The higher the score, the greater chance the relationship has to survive. We'll break it down below. Cross your fingers—good luck!

"A" GRADE: 150–130

If your Final Score is between 150 and 130 points, then your relationship's grade is between 100% and 91%, which is an "**A**" grade. This means that your relationship with your mate is in good standing, and neither of you have much to worry about! Congratulations! Both of you deserve a treat—and when it comes to treats, sooner is always better than later! Keep up the good work and be sure to sustain this high score, and your partnership is bound to flourish.

"B " GRADE: 129–100

If your Final Score is between 129 and 100 points, then your relationship's grade is between 90% and 85%. This is a "**B**" grade, which means your relationship needs some work. It is at risk of becoming weak due to a few areas of concern that need immediate attention. Check your scores on each test. The tests where you scored the lowest are the elements of ART that you need to focus on repairing. The next section ("Establishing and Strengthening ART") will give you valuable advice about improving those scores. Ignoring one of the elements or failing to repair it quickly can cause the other

ART elements to weaken or fall apart. If that happens, your relationship will steadily devolve and eventually fall apart.

"C" GRADE: 99–80

If your Final Score is in the 99 to 80 points, then your relationship's grade between 84% and 73%., which means you have a "**C**" grade. Read every page of this chapter, because your relationship is in serious trouble. It's been diagnosed with cancer; now give it the treatment it needs—**immediately**. Look closely at your test scores and identify the elements of ART where you scored the lowest. Do you understand why your score was so low? What can you do to fix these elements? The next section ("Establishing and Strengthening ART") will point you in the right direction, but you have to take your task very seriously. If you're unwilling to do the work, it might be time to go your separate ways.

"D" GRADE: 79 and Below

If your Final Score is 79 or less point, this means that your relationship is 74% of less, which is a "D" to "F" grade. Just skip "D" and go straight to "F," because **"D"** means your relationship is **Done**

"F" GRADE

If your Final Score is 79 or less, then you are at or below 74%. Your relationship is **"F"** grade, to be blunt, a failure. It lacks ART (Acceptance, Respect, and Trust), and it is not Actual Real True love. This relationship is most likely based on some kind of mutual benefit. If you aren't interested in finding Actual Real True love with your partner, then feel free to stay in this relationship and enjoy it. But if you want pure love and a permanent connection, than you need ART, and this relationship does not have it. It's time for you to think things through and move on. After all, you'd rather break up now than break down later.

Establishing and Strengthening ART

ART is the ultimate canvas for all successful relationships because it creates a rock-solid foundation upon which your bond can grow, be nourished, and come into full bloom. The lack of one or more elements of ART is what causes the downfall of most serious relationships. No couple can survive without it, because Actual Real True love cannot exist where there is no ART.

```
                Acceptance
        "In sickness and in health"   "Till death do us part"   Respect
                        LOVE
              "For richer or poorer"
                      Trust
```

ART in the Marriage Vows

Acceptance: **"For better or for worse, in sickness and in health…"** When you marry someone, you promise to accept every aspect of him or her, even if that aspect could be stronger. If your partner changes in some way, you accept his or her personal growth, even if you would have made different choices. To quote Shakespeare, "Love is not love which alters when it alteration finds."

Respect: **"From this day forward, until death do us part…"** Those who truly respect one another have faith that their bond is so strong that it will never be broken. Even after death parts you, you will remember your mate with great respect. You do not demean, belittle, or look down on any aspect of your partner; instead,

	you build one another up, helping each other reach your full potential.
Trust:	**"To love and to cherish, for richer or for poorer…"** No matter what life throws your way, you and your *JUST* Right partner will be able to handle it together. Your relationship will strengthen as the years pass, and you will always cherish each other as true mates.

When these three elements come together, you have attained **A**ctual **R**eal **T**rue love.

There is an "art" to reaching ART. When two people first meet, they must take the time to get to know one another in order to completely *accept* each other. Before you fully accept someone, you should not invite that person into your life. If you find that you cannot tolerate certain qualities, you need to move on.

The parties must also show *respect* to each other from the very beginning. As you discover each other, take their feelings into consideration and make them feel like a valued part of your life. Think before you speak, and let your love for each other (not your ego or your temper!) guide your words.

Last but not least, the couple must develop complete ***trust*** in order for the relationship to fully bloom. You and your mate will not last long if you feel like you must always be "on your toes" around each other, or if you feel like you must always keep an eye on a partner you cannot depend upon.

Once you have established all three ART elements in your relationship, you will know that you are *JUST* Right for each other. But never take these elements for granted once you know you have them. It takes vigilance to keep a relationship alive. The same techniques are suggested for both healing a relationship and keeping an existing relationship strong.

ARTistry: The Canvas of Love

Picture your relationship as a canvas. In your mind, you have an image of how you want the finished piece to look. You want to create a vivid painting that reflects warmth, caring, and devotion. You'll name it "The ART of Love."

In your relationship, both parties are ARTists. Plan your brush strokes well. Which images and colors do you want to add to your painting? You don't want to haphazardly throw paint on the canvas and hope it looks nice in the end. Instead, you want to create a vibrant, stunning masterpiece that will be admired by all as the years pass.

You want your friends to applaud you for your work of ART. You want your family to take joy in the painting you have created. You want future generations to remember and be inspired by your ARTwork. You want to display it to your children to show them what they should look for when they paint their own canvases.

So how do you get there? No matter how they chose to create and express love, artists are bound by certain rules. A painter needs particular tools, such as paint and a brush of some form. He must choose his brush, blend his paint, and apply the strokes to his canvas until his painting is complete.

Let's apply this to a relationship. Perhaps your goal as a "painter" is to create a canvas that involves children. You have decided to get married in order to have kids, maybe because you are growing older and feel like your time is running out. You're not looking for Prince Charming; you're simply looking for a good father for your children. When you build this relationship, choose the brush strokes that will create a happy home in which you can raise your family. Be honest with one another about your goals and **accept** each other's feelings and opinions on childrearing. **Respect** your partnership and the family you hope to build; never put it in second place. **Trust** each other to be good parents and role models for your children.

Creating a work of ART isn't a walk in the park. It takes hard work and perseverance. Most people would love to be ARTists, but not everyone is willing to apply themselves to creating a masterpiece. Unless you put in the time and effort, you will have nothing to hang on your wall. After all, you can't just take credit for a painting someone else has produced. Likewise, if you want a strong relationship, you have to invest time and effort into it in order to reap the benefits.

When Leonardo da Vinci created the *Mona Lisa*, he had to follow the same rules: using paint and a brush and carefully choosing the strokes he placed on his canvas. He didn't start smearing the paint around with no sense of purpose. Instead, he drew upon all of his skills as an artist to create one of the world's most famous portraits—one that has truly stood the test of time.

Like Leonardo, you possess certain skills. Perhaps you are a wonderful listener. Perhaps you are gifted at helping people grow spiritually. If you want your relationship to be the *Mona Lisa* of marriages, use all of these skills! Bring your best self to the battle! Show your spouse how good you are at listening to his or her dreams or fears. If your mate needs spiritual fulfillment, be a helpful guide along that path.

If your relationship is already anything like the *Mona Lisa*, then you have something worth fighting for. This means that your connection is unique, admirable, and complex. It may even seem confusing to others because they don't understand the components that make your partnership so beautiful, but they love what they see. No one knows what Lisa del Giocondo (whom most historians believe was Leonardo's model) was thinking while she posed for the portrait, but the mysterious beauty hidden in her unique smile captivates us to this day.

It's an ART, not a TA or a RA!

If any of the elements of the ART formula is missing, you have an incomplete canvas. You and your mate must to work hard to re-establish the missing piece immediately.

We're trying to create a work of ART, not a work of TA, RT, or RA! These three categories work together to build a strong foundation for a lasting relationship. Can you fully accept a person you don't trust or respect? Can you truly trust a person you don't respect or accept? Can you ever respect a person you don't accept or trust? Or can you fully love a person you don't accept, respect and trust?

When one of these elements falters, you have three choices:

Correct It,
Resign Yourself to It, or
Leave It.

How do you want to live your life? Do you want to just go through the motions, or do you want to be your best self? Do you want a stale relationship, or Actual Real True love?

A relationship is a living thing. It is constantly growing and changing. With ART, the two of you can grow together. But if one of these pieces falls out of alignment, it's as though a cancer has entered the union. It begins with a small **lump**—a minor kink that you might easily overlook. Left untreated, however, this lump will spread through the relationship, destroying healthy cells along the way. With any form of cancer, early treatment is imperative. You want to catch it at what doctors call "Stage Zero": its youngest, weakest form. Ignoring the problem doesn't make it go away; it just makes it harder to recover from the illness.

If two elements of ART are missing, your relationship is in Stage IV **cancer**: it has metastasized (i.e. spread) throughout the body. Death can come quickly and without warning. This relationship needs immediate and intensive attention. The parties involved have to be strong enough to fight the battle with great diligence, or their bond has no hope of survival.

Any relationship that lacks all three of the ART elements must be pronounced **dead**. –You aren't Jesus, and you can't raise the dead. It's time to "let the dead bury their own dead." You don't want to spend the rest of your days living in a grave. Holding on to a dead relationship will only destroy the parts of you that are still alive.

However … all is not lost. The human heart is a very complicated thing. Sometimes, when two people let go of a dead relationship, it helps them realize the value and importance of what they once had. They might begin to miss one another and desire each other again. As the old saying goes, "If you love something, set it free. If it comes back to you, it's yours; if it doesn't, it never was."

If this happens, take the opportunity to rebuild your relationship on the foundation of ART. Otherwise, you are doomed to make the same mistakes again. Accept each other as you truly are, respect one another as equal partners, and give each other the trust that will nourish your union. Paint a masterpiece that will catch people's breath.

CHAPTER SIX

CASE STUDIES

IN THE PREVIOUS chapters, you learned all about the science of identifying your Mr. or Ms. *JUST* Right. You established the qualities you seek in a mate, the age pairings that work best, and the elements of ART (Acceptance, Respect, and Trust) that make a relationship last. So what does this all look like when it comes together?

As we established in Chapter Two, **borrowed knowledge** is your best means of learning about romantic relationships. Remember, borrowed knowledge is information that you gather from the experiences of others. It isn't about what they tell you—it's about what they do. In that chapter, I recommended watching people's interactions (particularly those whose relationships you admire) and studying both the patterns that work for them and the patterns that don't.

While the best sources of borrowed knowledge are people that you know, respect, and trust, these patterns are playing out in relationships all across the world. Some of these couples are so famous that we all know the intimate details of their love lives. So let's study them together, and see what we can learn from these high-profile relationships.

Marc Anthony and Jennifer Lopez:
"Let's Just Make This Happen"

Marc Anthony was thirty-six years old when he married Jennifer Lopez (a.k.a. J.Lo) in June of 2004. She was thirty-five. Less than eight years later, they filed for divorce in April of 2012.

At thirty-six, Marc had just entered the "*Oh Snap*" state of mind; at thirty-five, J.Lo had finally realized that she was "*In Denial*"—and perilously close to "*Whatever!*" She knew she would have to settle in order to accomplish her goal of becoming a mother. For the sake of convenience, she accepted Marc because she saw him as a satisfactory candidate for fathering her children. He accepted her due to his desire for a companion and sexual partner.

The couple had actually known each other for more than a decade before they married. They met backstage at Paul Simon's 1998 Broadway show, "The Capeman." At that point, J.Lo was in her "*Innocence*" stage and her focus was on her career. Marc was "*Experimenting*" and had no idea where his life would take him. J.Lo had the power during their initial meeting, but she was just coming out of a divorce (she had been married to actor Ojani Noa for less than a year when they split in January of 1998) and wasn't looking for commitment. This "*Innocence*" and "*Experimenting*" had no chance of building a successful relationship at that point.

As we learned in Chapter Two, people are constantly moving in and out of Age Groups, and certain partners who don't meet our criteria at one stage in our lives might deserve a second look when we enter a different Age Group. When Marc Anthony and J.Lo finally exchanged vows, they knew each other's strengths and weaknesses and decided that they could fulfill each other's desires.

Their story is a classic example of the couple that decides to "just make this happen." Relationships like this can easily work out if both parties understand each other's needs and motivations, but only if the relationship is built on ART. The couple's failure—despite Marc Anthony's fulfillment of J.Lo's need for children—indicates that at least one element of ART was missing.

Advice for Marc

Marc, even though you are in the "*Oh Snap!*" stage of your life, you have all of the assets you need to attract a woman from any Age Group: money, fame, power, and lifestyle. We know that it's only a matter of time until you open yourself up to a new relationship.

So don't worry too much about being too old. Remember the rest of the "*Oh Snap!*" motto: "No money, no honey." You have plenty of money, so honey won't be in short supply. Just remember that "*Innocence*" will want you only for your assets, "*In Denial*" may or may not view you as an equal, and "*Whatever!*" probably won't interest you unless she brings significant assets, such as beauty and fame, into the relationship.

Advice for J.Lo

J.Lo, I understand your motivations. You're now forty-three and in the "*Whatever!*" state of mind, and you've decided to have some fun with Casper Smart, who is only twenty-five. This aptly-named "*Experimenting*" is being quite *smart* by dating you. He's open to any relationship, and you're the perfect pick for him. You are increasing his fame and standing—and therefore his power when he becomes "*The Catch*" in a few short months—while giving him a mother figure who can lavish him with affection, approval, and gifts. And I'm sure he's enjoying your time in the bedroom!

You're in a temporary relationship, and you probably know it. He probably knows it, too. Mr. Smart will soon come into his power when he becomes the ultimate "Catch." He will then move on to a woman he has chosen.

J.Lo, you have a decision to make. Will you continue to use your money, power, fame, and opportunities to move from one temporary relationship to another? Your assets are getting you what you want, and you're having a lot of fun with younger men. We have only one life to live, and there's nothing wrong with enjoying it!

But if you're looking for a permanent relationship, remember that time is passing, and you won't always be as beautiful as you are today. A woman in the "*Whatever!*" state of mind commits to a man for two reasons: companionship and predictability. Your best bet is to use your remaining youth to catch "*The Catch.*" He can still be molded and shaped into the JUST Right mate, but he has come into his full power. He knows what he wants and where he's going. With "*Experimenting,*" you would have to invest a great deal of time into his development. And a man in your Age Group may be panicking ("*Oh Snap!*") and need a significant amount of patience and assurance from his partner as he comes to terms with his social standing and his physical and mental state. If you're willing to do the work to reach ART with "*The Catch,*" you'll get the companionship you need with a man who can be anything you want him to be.

President and First Lady Obama:
"Moving On Up With the Right Partner."

President Barack Obama was nowhere near making history as the first black president of the United States when he met his future First Lady, Michelle Robinson, at the end of his first year at Harvard Law School. And this influential couple still had no idea what was in store for them when they got married in 1992. Together, they would make an unstoppable team.

Michelle was twenty-eight years old when they exchanged vows, and Mr. Obama was thirty-one. At that point, Michelle was at the "*In Denial*" stage, while her "Catch" knew exactly what he wanted and how to get it. He understood that he needed a partner, not a trophy wife. He therefore chose a fully educated, strong, and highly intelligent woman as his mate.

Michelle knew the man she had fallen in love with was destined for great things—very great things, as it turned out! —and that many other women wanted to "catch" him. She chose wisely in accepting him for a mate, and her decision has brought her name into the history books.

A "Marriage of True Minds"

In this marriage, both parties complete each other and bring balance to one another. Whatever one spouse is lacking, the other fills. These two bright, accomplished people can relate to one another as equal partners. Both of them have the same agenda, family goals, career objectives, and love for their country. Their marriage is highly likely to succeed because President Obama chose her after reaching his full power, at a time when he had many other choices. He knew she was the one for him, and he will remain dedicated to keeping her happy.

MR. OR MS. JUST RIGHT

Advice for President Obama

President Obama, not only did you make history, but you also chose the right partner to share your journey. You know that a man who is on a journey needs a partner, a man who seeks contentment needs a wife, and a man who wants to stay grounded needs children. When you met the woman who could give you all of these things, you were smart enough to seal the deal. You got a partner with the same life journey as you, a wife to keep you content and focused, and children who will keep you grounded so you never forget were you came from. Always treat them with Acceptance, Respect, and Trust, and your journey will be a very happy one.

Advice for Mrs. Obama

Michelle, you have truly found a good man. He may not be perfect—no man is! But he understands the importance of getting what he wants and knows how to use his power and his talents to pursue what his heart desires.

Your "Catch" is now in the "*Oh Snap!*" state of mind, but you need not worry! He chose you because you fulfill and complete him in the most important areas of his life and his heart. He made that choice because he knew you were everything he was lacking and that he could give you everything you needed. The moment he gave his heart to you, he decided that you were the only one for him. He will now put in the effort that it takes to make you happy throughout your life.

Your mate will always keep other women at least an arm's length away from him, or even farther. Continue maintaining the ART in your marriage, and the two of you will continue to cherish each other throughout your lives.

Prince William and Kate Middleton:
"The Prince and the (Patient) Peasant"

On November 16, 2010, people around the world were glued to their television screens. Prince William, Duke of Cambridge, was taking the hand of Kate Middleton (now known as Catherine, Duchess of Cambridge) in marriage. Both were twenty-eight years old when they wed.

Before this fairytale wedding took place, the couple met at the University of St. Andrews in 2001, when both of them were nineteen. At that point, Kate was in the "*Innocence*" Age Group and Prince William was still "*Experimenting*." Neither of them was thinking about marriage, but Kate had the power in their dynamic and she knew how to use it to her greatest advantage.

She was dating a young man who had power over everything around him except for the one thing that he couldn't control: love. Kate understood that she had to be patient with her prince until he came into his full power as "*The Catch*" and was able to choose her. At that point, he would know what he wanted—and she made sure what he wanted was her.

Shifting Power Can Strengthen a Relationship

Because Kate chose William when they began dating, but allowed him to choose her for marriage, this couple's union has a high chance of succeeding. Both partners have chosen each other at different times in their lives. They both made that choice; so they will both try their best to make the marriage work. I predict that this royal couple will be a household name for decades to come.

Advice for Prince William

William, you may be one of the most powerful men in the world, but your life will be meaningless without your Actual Real True love. You and Kate chose each other at the right times, and your relationship will remain rock solid if you always Accept, Respect, and Trust one another. When you hit the "*Oh Snap*" zone, please remember that nothing else and no one else can compare to the woman of your dreams. Always show her that you cherish her, and your marriage will always be a true gift.

Advice for Kate

Kate, be aware that your prince might panic when he reaches the third Age Group ("*Oh Snap!*") out of fear of growing old. His behavior might change for the worse during this period. But stay strong; as long as you have put in the work to maintain ART in your marriage, it will pass. You may have chosen him at the beginning of the relationship, but he chose you for marriage at the peak of his power. That means that he is willing to do whatever it takes to please you.

No matter what he does, just remember that he will always come back home to you. He made up his mind to share his life with you when he chose you out of the countless women who wanted him. He would not have done so unless he knew your relationship was built upon Acceptance, Respect, and Trust. Keep up the good work with these elements, and he will always be your prince.

Ellen DeGeneres and Portia de Rossi:
"Leading by Example"

The principles of ART aren't just for male–female romantic relationships! They apply equally well to relationships of all kinds, including marriages between same-sex partners. And the characteristics of the female Age Groups apply to all women, regardless of their sexual orientation. When it comes down to it, we're all quite similar in the most fundamental aspects of our lives.

Ellen and Portia met backstage at an awards show in 2004, and quickly fell in love. They exchanged vows in August of 2008. Ellen was fifty years old—in the "*Whatever!*" state of mind—and her bride was in her final year of being "*In Denial*" at thirty-five.

At that point in her life, Ellen was looking for companionship and a satisfying sexual relationship with a beautiful younger woman. Portia knew she was on the verge of hitting the "*Whatever!*" stage, and was ready to accept a mate before she passed her prime. But she was still in the second age bracket, and Ellen was fifteen years older than her. That large age gap gave Portia the power in the relationship, as we discussed in the "*Whatever!*" section of Chapter Three.

In essence, she chose Ellen, because Portia had more options open to her. But since they both brought assets, such as wealth, social standing, and fame, into the relationship, they were able to come together as equal partners. Four years later, they are still going strong, and I predict a very happy future for this ground-breaking couple!

Advice for Ellen

Ellen, you have a lovely, talented woman at your side! Take advantage of all of the benefits that she brings. She will give you companionship and comfort as you get older, and she will always be young in your eyes. Make sure you nurture her and keep her needs in mind. We know how much you love dancing, so be her dance partner for life. It's like opening the car door for your date—once you start; you need to keep it up. Don't stop doing the little things that make her happy as time passes. Even if you're ninety-six years old, try dancing the two-step with your cane!

As Portia ages, she might panic over the loss of her youth, but be patient with her. She chose you while she still had many other options, and she is committed to building a lasting relationship with you.

Advice for Portia

Portia, you have chosen very well! By accepting Ellen into your life, you gained a nurturing partner who will spoil you and lavish you with affection. Her assets are the source of her power, and she has plenty of them. Enjoy your life together! Just remember not to do anything that might threaten your relationship if you start feeling anxious about getting older. Ride it out, and always work on preserving the Acceptance, Respect, and Trust you have in your marriage. If you do, the two of you will continue to be an inspiration all others who are trying to identify their sexuality.

Nicholas Cannon and Mariah Carey:
"When a Man Loves a Woman"

This couple first met at the 2005 Billboard Music Awards, when Nick Cannon gave the award for Best Selling Female Artist of the Year to Mariah Carey. Who would've guessed that just three years later they would be married?

On April 30, 2008, the couple was wed at Mariah's private estate on Windermere Island in the Bahamas. They

MR. OR MS. JUST RIGHT

had been dating for only six weeks before they got married! But you never know when, where, or how quickly you will find love. You might meet your Mr. *JUST* Right at the fair while he spills his lemonade all over your shirt. That's why it's important to always put your best self forward and be ready to accept the right mate.

On their wedding day, Nick was twenty-eight years old—"T*he Catch*"—and had all the power. His bride, Mariah, was thirty-eight, and was in the "*Whatever!*" state of mind. She accepted the choice of her "Catch" because she felt he would complete her. Since Nick had many other choices but sealed the deal with the woman his heart desired, this marriage got off to a very strong start. If they maintain the Acceptance, Respect, and Trust that they have for one another, their union will be a success.

Finding Mr. **JUST** *Right after Ditching Mr. Wrong*

Although Nick is not Mariah's first husband, he could easily be her first (and last!) Actual Real True love. Mariah married him shortly after entering the "*Whatever!*" state of mind. She was exhausted by the wild goose chase of searching for Mr. Right, and had realized that her White Knight probably wasn't going to come along after all. Just in the *nick* of time, her Mr. *JUST* Right chose her, filling in the parts of her life that needed fulfillment.

Nick knew the power he possessed as "*The Catch*," and he knew how to pursue the one and only woman of his dreams. He chose her because he wanted a soul mate, a partner, and a lover, as well as the affection and comfort of a mature woman with whom he could build a marriage based on Acceptance, Respect, and Trust.

Advice for Nick

Nick, you have it all, and you know and appreciate the power of having it all. Enjoy it, embrace it, and always give thanks for it. When you find yourself in the "*Oh Snap*" state of mind, try hard to be content and not risk the love you share with your wife. What you have now is more than most men could ever dream of having, so hold on to it. Your wife has made you whole, and if you cherish her and stay true to her, she will always keep you fulfilled.

Advice for Mariah

Mariah, congratulations! You were strong enough and genuine enough to make this very eligible "Catch." As he gets older, he will eventually enter the "*Oh Snap!*" age bracket. Forgive him now for the things he might do then to boost his assurance that he's still "got it." When that day comes, remember that you have nothing to do with the panic he might experience. The best thing you can do to help him is to allow him to get through that crisis without judging him or threatening him with divorce.

I know that living a high-profile lifestyle as a celebrity is exhausting, and that you always have to stay on your toes. If Nick acts out as he approaches or reaches the next Age Group, you may feel very tempted to leave him so your fans won't think you are weak or have lost your confidence and self-esteem. My advice to you is to shock the world and meet this challenge like a mature woman. Hold your head high, and hold on to the ART you have built with Nick, and your love will last you a lifetime.

Ashton Kutcher and Demi Moore:
"A Trail of Broken Hearts"

In 2003, Ashton was twenty-five years old and discovering himself ("*Experimenting*") when he began dating Demi Moore, who was officially in the "*Whatever!*" state of mind at the age of forty. When they got married in September of 2005, he had attained his full power as "T*he Catch*" and had all of the assets he needed to choose any woman he wanted. Their marriage was doomed from the start for a number of reasons.

After her thirteen-year marriage to Bruce Willis ended in 2000, Demi lost touch with herself. Bruce and Demi had married while she was in the "*Innocence*" age bracket at the age of twenty and he was "*The Catch*" at the age of thirty. Both had power when they entered into a marriage of equals based on Acceptance, Respect, and Trust, and they were able to find Actual Real True love with each other. Somewhere along the way, they lost one or more of the elements of ART. Bruce entered the "*Oh Snap!*" state of mind, which is a time when men's behavior often changes for the worse. "*In Denial*" Demi freaked out and thought she still held the power of an "*Innocence*" over him. The cancer of a missing ART element invaded their marriage and destroyed it from within.

When Ashton accepted Demi as his wife, he was most likely looking for a convenient source of attention, flattery, and comfort. She also offered a means of expanding his opportunities, fame, and assets. He had only recently become "*The Catch*," and perhaps felt like he needed a mother figure until he sorted out his life. Demi had already lost Bruce, her Actual Real True love, and was ready to accept anyone in her "*Whatever!*" stage. Their relationship had no hope of establishing Acceptance, Respect, and Trust. By the time the couple divorced in 2011, this "Catch" was ready to exert his full power and knew he had limited time to choose the woman he fully desired—not the woman he had accepted for the sake of convenience.

Advice for Ashton

Ashton, you will undoubtedly remarry, but think carefully about the woman you choose. You are now thirty-five years old, and in your final year as "*The Catch*." Take advantage of it! You have full power over "*In Denial*," but you also have other options. At this age, you can still attract "*Innocence*" without relying on your assets, and you can still shape her into the woman you want her to be.

Once you cross into "*Oh Snap!*" territory, you might find yourself back in divorce court if you marry "*In Denial*," because she will always think that she chose you—which will make her fight you for the power in your relationship, even though she doesn't really have it. If you marry "*Innocence*," you must remember that she is will be choosing you solely for what you have to offer: your money, fame, and lifestyle. The good news is that she will be compliant and moldable—and very fun in the bedroom! If you find another woman in the "*Whatever!*" state of mind while you are in the "*Oh Snap!*" zone, you may meet each other as equals, and your marriage will succeed if you exercise ART at all times.

Advice for Demi

Demi, Ashton may have broken your heart, but it is better to get out of a dead-end relationships sooner rather than later. You're still beautiful, and you haven't started cashing your social security checks just yet. You are comfortable with your body, you still have plenty of stamina, and you have many assets to offer. This means you can catch another "Catch," but it will only work if base your relationship on Acceptance, Respect, and Trust. Remember that he will have the power in your relationship, and don't challenge him for it. Let him be a man.

"*Experimenting*" is a bad choice for you—don't make the same mistake twice! He may accept you now, but once he reaches the age of "*The Catch*," he might quickly realize that he wants to choose a partner who will make him feel like he's in control of things.

Think long and hard about your relationship with Bruce. You may think the two of you are through with each other, but a new beginning could be waiting for you. The respect with which you have treated each other since your divorce speaks volumes about the love that you still share. Bruce married Emma Heming in 2009, when she was thirty-two, was "*In Denial*," and probably thought she had the power in their relationship. But you may well be Bruce's only Actual Real True love, which means that Emma doesn't have the control she thinks she has. She is right about to hit the "*Whatever!*" stage, and unless they have full ART in their marriage, things could quickly fall apart. She may realize she lacks control and try to find it with a younger man.

You and Bruce chose each other when you were both in your full power as "*Innocence*" and "*The Catch*." That mutual selection is a very potent thing, and you went on to fulfill each other's desires and to groom, mold, and shape each other for thirteen years! That bond will never fully break. If the two of you find your way back together, make sure you constantly pay attention to all of the elements of ART, and you will be in bliss with your Actual Real True love.

But if you never reunite with Bruce, you have to remember that other men in his Age Group will likely want you only for your assets. You probably have much more to offer than other men of your age, so be careful with the "*Oh Snap!*" bracket. He may be focusing on what you can do for him, not what he can do for you. And if his assets exceed yours, he may wake up one day and decide he needs a younger woman to make him feel young again.

And Some Advice for Emma, Too!

Emma, now is the time when you must be careful. Bruce was in an "*Oh Snap!*" (i.e. panicked) state of mind and was still mourning his lost love with Demi when the two of you got married. You are "*In Denial*" if you think that you chose him and control this relationship. To make this marriage last, you must focus on fulfilling his needs and desires that became empty when he divorced Demi. Remember, the bond between those two will never be broken, and you don't want to drive him back into her arms. Accept the fact that you no longer have the power of "*Innocence*," and make Bruce feel like a man who is in control of his home. As long as you remember to cherish each other through the ART of Acceptance, Respect, and Trust, you will always have him to yourself.

FINAL THOUGHTS

TIME WAITS FOR no man—or woman! You have read this book and discovered the power of your Age Group. Now go use it!

It is always in your best interests to know where you stand and to be ready to accept your Mr. or Ms. *JUST* Right. You may be having fun right now, but your days of fun are numbered. At some point, you will lose the power you possess today, and you can never get it back. So take a good look at yourself, assess your strengths and weaknesses, and put your new knowledge to good use.

Remember to start by setting all of your fairy-tale notions on fire. This is reality, and we're going to face it like realistic men and women. Those silly ideas are preventing you from accepting your true mate, so send them packing.

Every single person who has read this book should have a list of the qualities that you seek in a mate committed to memory. If your memory isn't that great, put your list on your fridge! Frame it and hang it over your desk! Do whatever it takes to keep your list at the front of your mind. Whenever you meet prospective partners, assess them honestly and make sure they meet at least most of those qualities. If not, your relationship will be a temporary one. You can accept that now and walk away without a broken heart, or you can drag yourself through a divorce later. The choice is yours.

Identify your Age Group and the age brackets of the people you meet. Don't fool yourself—feeling young doesn't make you young! That lovely "*Innocence*" at the bar doesn't believe for one second that the "*Oh Snap!*" hitting on her is her Prince Charming. And the juicy "*Experimenting*" you meet on the dance floor may be interested in sleeping with "*Whatever!*" but he knows you're past your prime, even if you haven't figured it out yet. Please don't make a fool of yourself.

Once you know the Age Group and required qualities of your perfect match, you will have narrowed down a gigantic dating pool into a manageable group of prospective partners. While everyone who *hasn't* read this book will be making mistakes right and left, you'll be focused on your goals and you'll know how to reach them.

Of course, there are exceptions to every rule. Although the age pairings in this book work in the vast majority of cases, human beings always have the capacity to surprise us. Sometimes, the long shots come in. Just stay realistic. If you feel like you're jamming a square peg into a round hole, try looking for a square hole instead.

And don't forget that our ages are always changing. You may meet your Mr. or Ms. *JUST* Right at a time when your age brackets aren't compatible. But a few years might make a world of difference. That "Experimenter" you dismissed might become "*The Catch*" right before your eyes. If an opportunity opens up, seize it! Try to forgive past mistakes—just laugh at them and learn from them.

When you do find the *JUST* Right relationship (or if you are lucky enough to be in it now!), nurture it with **Acceptance**, **Respect**, and **Trust**. Cherish your partner. Accept each other fully into your lives, and give each other the support and compassion that everyone needs from their Actual Real True love.

Love is life's greatest gift, so go find it. Paint your masterpiece!

And remember: Always wear clean undies; you never know when you'll get hit by a bus!

GLOSSARY

Acceptance |ak´-sept-əns| *noun*: approval or favorable regard.

Actual |´ak-choō-əl| *adjective*: existing in fact; typically as contrasted with what was intended, expected, or believed.

A.R.T (*acronym*): Acceptance, Respect, and Trust.

Artist |´är-tist| *noun*: a person who produces paintings or drawings as a profession or hobby.

Cohabit |kō-´ha-bit| *verb*: to live together and have a sexual relationship without being married.

Damage |´dam-ij| *noun:* harm caused to something in such a way as to impair its value, usefulness, or normal function.

Death |deθ| *noun*: the action or fact of dying or being killed; the end of the life of a person or organism.

Guardian |´gär-dē-ən| *noun*: a defender, protector, or keeper.

Gusto |ˈgə-stō| *noun*: enjoyment or vigor in doing something; zest.

Health |helθ| *noun*: the state of being free from illness or injury.

Idealism |ī-ˈdē-(ə)-ˌliz-əm| *noun*: the practice of forming or pursuing ideals, especially unrealistically.

***JUST* Right** |jəst| |rīt| *compound adjective*: perfectly suited to a particular purpose or person.

Love |ləv| *noun*: an intense feeling of deep affection through the expression of Acceptance, Respect, and Trust (ART).

Melancholy |ˈmel-ən-ˌkä-lē| *noun*: a deep, pensive, and long-lasting sadness.

Negotiation |nə-ˌgō-SHē-ˈā-SHən| *noun*: discussion aimed at reaching an agreement.

Rationalism |ˈra-shə-nəl-ˌiz-əm| *noun*: a belief or theory that opinions and actions should be based on reason and knowledge rather than on religious belief or emotional response.

Real |ˈrē(ə)l| *adjective*: actually existing as a thing or occurring in fact; not imagined or supposed.

Realism |ˈrē-ə-ˌli-zəm| *noun*: the attitude or practice of accepting a situation as it is and being prepared to deal with it accordingly.

Respect |ri-ˈspekt| *noun*: due regard for the feelings, wishes, rights, or traditions of others.

Sickly |ˈsik-lē| *adjective*: often ill; in poor health.

True |troō| *adjective*: loyal or faithful.

Trust |trəst| *noun*: firm belief in the reliability, truth, ability, or strength of someone or something.

Vigilance |ˈvi-jəl-əns| *noun*: the action or state of keeping careful watch for possible danger or difficulties.

AUTHOR BIO

OPRAH WINFREY GRADUATED from the Academy of Art University in San Francisco, California, and now resides in North Carolina with her family. As a mother, homemaker, published author, inspirational speaker, motivational figure, artist, entrepreneur, and lover of life, she makes sure the brush strokes on the canvas of her life are filled with beauty.

Her many years of working in the beauty industry gave Oprah the perfect opportunity to observe relationships—especially romantic ones. She quickly recognized that many of her clients had the same goals and questions: "I want to find Mr. Right!" "How do you know if someone is Ms. Just Right?" "What is pure love?" "Does Mr. Right really exist?"

Inspired by these questions, Oprah kept a diary of both these interactions and the conversations she had with clients that shed light on a relationship's chances of survival. She saw a very clear pattern emerge, and her observations culminated in the advice that this book offers.

Oprah gives special thanks to the one and only Creator of all things; to her clients for all of the joy that they have brought her as they gossiped, shared, and imagined with her; and to her family for molding her into a woman who can recognize wisdom when she sees it.

CPSIA information can be obtained
at www.ICGtesting.com
Printed in the USA
LVOW04s0054221016
509645LV00011B/128/P